THE MAN WHO STOLE THE WORLD CUP

WRITTEN BY
JOHN J. MACHIN

WITH
PAUL J. MACHIN

EDITED BY
LAUREN MACHIN

Second Edition: Printed 2024 by the Machin Family.
This Book exists because of the generosity of the 546 people who backed it on Kickstarter. Heroes.

For the latest "Man Who..." Updates, follow:
x.com/ManWhoStoleBook

For Media or General enquiries contact:
themanwhostolebook@gmail.com

This book is a work of fiction. Unless otherwise indicated, all the names, characters, businesses, places, events and incidents in this book are either the product of the author's imagination or used in a fictitious manner. This is especially true, but in totally different ways, of Kenny Dalglish (Legend), Spider-man (God if only we'd created him!) and Pickles (Wonderdog).

"For Annette, who else?"

- John J. Machin

CHAPTER ONE:

KENNY DALGLISH & THE AMAZING SPIDER-MAN

Friday. 4th April 1986. 12:38pm. Liverpool.

"If you could make a wish, what would it be?" The teenage girl asked as she finished pulling a pink plastic comb through her thick, shoulder length brown hair. She tied it up into a high ponytail using a bright, aqua blue scrunchy, all the while staring out of the bus window, as if uninterested in the answer.

"I thought you always got three wishes?" The young boy suggested, fidgeting on the cold vinyl seat. "I read this comic once where this astronaut landed on…"

"Alright, THREE then." This time Jo turned away from her condensation-obscured view of the outside world to look at him. "Three wishes Andy. What are they?"

"It's sound, I only need one," Andy said cheerfully.

"I wish I had super powers."

"Superpowers?!" Jo's voice rose with incredulity and rang around the top deck. At the front of the bus an elderly lady with a paisley patterned head scarf half turned her head back towards the pair, 'harrumphed' in annoyance, and tucked her polythene shopping bag closer to her on the seat. Jo winced, and though she couldn't make it out, was convinced that the old dear was muttering something derogatory about them under her breath. She resolved to keep her voice down. Andy however met her tone and ran with it, standing up, and speaking with his hands to further illustrate his impassioned response.

"Yeah! What's wrong with that?? I'd be dead strong, and I'd be able to fly, or jump tall buildings, or climb walls…" He jumped onto the metal bar top of the seat next to them, wobbled slightly, and grabbed the vertical bar for balance. The old woman shifted round in her seat again, Jo's eyes widened in horror, "Andy get off there you little idiot!" She reached out to pull him down, but he skillfully sidestepped and swung acrobatically to the seat across the aisle.

"... I'd be able to read minds, " he continued, putting his right hand to his temple, and his left outstretched in front, "and make people do whatever I want," he pretended to focus, closing his eyes and pointing towards the disgruntled pensioner currently glowering at them from behind her horn rimmed spectacles. "I command you to stop being such a miserable old busybody," he said in a voice much deeper than his own. Jo gritted her teeth. Andy opened one eye to see if his word had any effect, and was met only by the woman's continued death stare. Andy wiggled his fingers and tilted his head back, "I command THEEEEE". The woman let out another large "harrumph," scooped up her bag, and walked down the stairs to the bottom deck. Jo couldn't contain herself any longer, and let out a snort of laughter.

"Andy, you little devil, pack it in, will ye? You're crackers!"

"No am not," Andy said, with a touch of hurt in his voice. He wiped away a wide smear of condensation with his forearm from the window. I'd be able to do whar'ever I wanted, go anywhere, no school, no parents, no care workers... and, and I'd be famous too, yeah, the most famous person in history!" He paused. "What about you?"

"Me?" Said Jo with mock surprise. "Oh I wish I was Kenny Dalglish, the best footballer in the world." She stated with a hint of pride and defiance.

"Eurgh, Kenny Dogfish? Not a horrible red, that's like me asking for superpowers and choosing to be Doctor Doom, or, or... the Green Goblin! And anyway, you can't be him, you're a girl!"

"So?" She glared at him. "What's that got to do with it? I'm better at footy than you are, than you'll ever be."

"No yer not, i've played for our school team!" Andy protested.

"Get lost! They don't have school teams that young.

"Yeah they do, and I'm eleven.:

"No they don't and you're not."

"They do and I will be next week. What would you know about it anyway, you're only a..." Andy was about to add again that she was only a girl, but seeing the aggression on her face thought better of it. Jo was less thoughtful.

"They certainly don't have any teams in that Remand Home you're in anyhow," she sneered and added, "I can play better than anyone in my school." She looked wistfully out of the window. "They keep getting beat," she said. "And they still don't play me!" Her disgust was clear. "Now if I was Kenny they'd be begging me,"

"Oh don't start that again," Andy sighed.

"I'm serious."

"Yeah sure."

"Honest. Haven't you ever wished you could be someone else- just so you could show people?"

"Yes."

"Well?"

"Well what?"

"Well who?"

"Peter Parker."

"Peter Parker? Who's he when he's at home?"

"Peter Parker, the Amazing Spider-man!" Andy announced dramatically.

"Spider-man? SPIDER? MAN?! Jo laughed. "You must be joking."

"No I'm not, it's no worse than a girl wanting to be Kenny Dalglish!"

"Don't start me," Jo stabbed the handle of the comb at Andy's shoulder.

"Well it's not!"

"But the Whatsits Spider-bloke? He's not even real!"

"What's that got to do with it? Besides, he's more real than the other super heroes. He's got problems with his aunt who he lives with, and with his girlfriend and everything. Just like anyone. But he's also got this power 'cause he was bitten by a radioactive spider. He can climb walls and swing around the city on his webbin'..." Andy paused for breath, "and he's always catching colds and getting beaten up and…"

"I thought superheroes caught baddies, not colds!" Jo interrupted, smiling.

"Yeah, yeah dead funny." Andy pulled a face and continued. "He always wins in the end and all the people who think he's little and puny…"

"Like you?" Jo laughed.

"Shurrup! Anyway no-one suspects who he really is, except for his girlfriend's dad but he gets killed when Doc Octopus drops a brick wall on him and Gwen, that's the girlfriend, she thinks Spidey did it and hates him 'cause she doesn't know he's really…"

"Okay, okay, I get the picture," said Jo, interrupting the torrent.

"So he's got problems. But Kenny really IS real, He's realer than your Spider-fella."

"More real," Andy corrected.

"What?"

"More real, not 'realer'."

"Alright smart-aleck, more real."

"But you're never going to be him are you? I mean girls don't play football."

"Yes they do. There's womens' teams all over Europe. They even play in the same stadiums as the mens' teams and they earn lots of money."

"Go 'way!" Andy said incredulously.

"They do. AND most of the best women players are from England, like me. There aren't many teams here so they have to go abroad. That's what I'm going to do. I'm gonna go to Italy and play in Rome where the glorious Reds won two European Cups." She said, with a dreamy look on her face. "I'm gonna be the female Kenny Dalglish. Where are you gonna find a radioactive spider?!" Jo laughed again.

"Go on laugh! Stranger things 'ave 'appened!" Andy insisted and brushed his hand across his bristly crew cut. "They 'appen all the time."

"Like what?"

"Flyin' saucers for one. Aliens from Outer Space."

"Get away. You don't believe in that rubbish do yer?"

"Yeah! It's a well known fact," Andy said authoritatively. "The army just keep the evidence a secret so as not to scare people."

"Behave!" Jo sneered, but there was doubt in her voice.

"My Aunty saw one by Page Moss shops, she told me, and not long after that our teacher told us that she had seen the same one, so it must be true!"

"Honest?" The mention of adults added weight to the story.

"Yeah," Andy continued, "there's nothing to stop us seeing one right now."

"Oh, you don't think we will do ye'?" Jo grabbed the boy's arm and peered out at the sky. "I'd die".

"There are loads of stories of people being taken up into space crafts and the aliens experimenting on them. Weeks later they turn up and have radiation burns all over them and don't remember anything until they're hypnotised."

"Oooh! That's horrible," Jo shivered and squirmed visibly,

"Fancy having slimy hands all over you. Urgh!"

"They're not slimy!" Andy said indignantly. "They're like us only either shorter or much taller depending on which kind they are. Now, if one came here and tried to use its tractor beam to raise us up into the ship, but the machine broke down so that we blinked in and out of our space and time and then got left behind as the saucer escaped, I could end up with all sorts of powers… So could you."

Jo paused for a moment and shook her head. "Nah, I'd defo rather be Kenny Dalglish, you've been reading too many of them comics." she said, getting to her feet abruptly. "Anyway, this is my stop."

They left the bus together and as they dodged their way through the lunchtime city crowds, Andy found himself a step behind, watching his companion. She was dressed in a dark blue leather jacket with elasticated cuffs, jeans with one inch turn-ups and a deep red blouse with all but its pointed collar hidden by a pale brown knitted jumper. Low heeled, shiny black shoes completed the outfit. She carried a rolled up magazine in her right hand, which accentuated the downward punching motion she made alternately with each fist as she walked. This affected movement made it more of a strut than a walk. Full of pride and arrogance, but also, as was shown by the little skips she made as she left or climbed a kerb, full of joy. When she reached a stretch of wasteland strewn with obstacles, broken bricks, stones and rubbish, she appeared to dance her way through them. When they were back in a crowded street, she glided past people like a silky winger, with small drops of the shoulder and turns of the hip. Andy, less graceful, gave a bumbling skip and a hop and landed beside her.

"I collect them," he announced.
"What?" Jo looked bewildered.
"Comics."
"Comics?"
"Yeah."
"What for?"

"Because I like them," Andy explained. "And they're worth lots of money."

"What do you mean? Like old footy programmes?"

"Yeah, only better. A Spider-man Number One costs as much as £200."

"You're joking! Two hundred quid!?" Jo lost Andy in the crowd momentarily. "Have you got one?"

"No," he reappeared. "No such luck. I've got them all from number 121 when Gwen gets killed by the Green Goblin."

"You what?"

"Gwen, Gwen Stacey, I told you, Spidey's girlfriend."

"Spare me the details," Jo said haughtily. "How much is that one worth?"

"Oh, about £6."

"You paid £6? For a comic??"

"No. I only paid about 10p for it in a junk shop," Andy explained proudly.

"Wow!" Jo was actually impressed. "When are you selling it?"

"Sell it!?" Andy was clearly shocked by the idea. "I'm not gonna sell it!

"Well, what's the point then?" Jo was clearly perplexed.

"Point? There isn't one. I just like comics, I told you. besides, I wanna get all of them first, all of Spider-man I mean."

"Huh. I always heard that you were a bit of a brain box. Can't see it myself, you're daft." Jo shook her head. "Comics!"

"That's why I did a runner from the Assessment Centre."

"You did what?" Jo stopped in her tracks. "You're on the run??"

"Yeah. There's a Comic Mart in London tomorrow. I've gorra go to. They don't have them in Liverpool anymore and they're bound to have loads of old Spideys," Andy tried to explain.

"I thought you said they were expensive," Jo asked, her suspicions raised. "Where are you getting the money?"

"Well, somethin' will come up."

"Somethin' will come up." She mimicked, and gave him a punch on the arm. "Isn't stealing what got you locked up in the first place?"

"Yeah, well?" Andy shrugged, "what can they do to me now?"

"And how exactly are you getting down there? It's two hundred miles away."

"I thought I'd go with you."
Jo stopped dead in her tracks. "Me?" She said incredulously.

"Yeah. You're going the match aren't you?"

"So?"

"The Semi-Final of the F.A Cup," Andy said theatrically,

"Liverpool versus Southampton, White Hart Lane, Tottenham, London. Kenny Dalglish."

Jo threw her hands in the air, and started walking again. Andy fell into step behind her.

"I should have known it was no coincidence you bumping into me like this!" She seethed. "The answer is no!"

"Pleeeease!" Andy pleaded.

"No! There is no way I'm going to help you bunk on My coach to London. Me Dad would murder me!"

"It's alright," Andy explained. "I've got money, I just want someone to go with. The bizzies are sure to pick me up if they see me on my own. Your mate Sandra in the corner shop told me you were going down to the coach station this morning to book the tickets for you and your Dad. If I book at the same time it won't look suspicious. I could even sit next to you."

Jo sighed.

"Wellll…"

"Go onnnn…" Andy pleaded, "pleeeeease?"

"Oh alright."

"YESSSSS!" Andy celebrated, punching both fists into the air.

"Me Dad and Uncle always ignore me anyway." Jo continued. "At least it'll give me someone to talk to, though what I'm going to talk to a ten year old kid about I don't know."

THE MAN WHO STOLE THE WORLD CUP

CHAPTER TWO:

THE SCAVENGER

<u>Saturday. 5th April 1986. 6:50am.</u>

Jo always felt queasy if she had to wake up early, out of her usual routine, especially if she had something different like travelling to do. Beneath the seat belt across her lap, she felt the excitement tingling in her stomach. Letting the cold air from the slightly opened car window play on her face, she concentrated on keeping her head perfectly still, looking out at the passing streets as they whipped past.
As her Father and Uncle chatted in the front seats about the prospective football game, her mother's voice droned on beside her in the back seat. Words - "careful, Dad, trouble, stay close, food" only vaguely penetrated Jo's consciousness as St. John's Beacon appeared on the skyline, and Liverpool City Centre unfolded before her.

She wondered why her mother hadn't driven. It would've made more sense.

"I'll just pull up here," her Dad said over his shoulder, as the back of the coach station appeared ahead of them. "This'll do".

Jumping out, Jo pulled her shell suit jacket around her.

A Christmas present from her uncle, and her pride and joy, the purple and green slashes of colour on the black top stood in contrast to her pale blue Levi's and pristine white Reebok high tops. With her hair tied up with a matching purple scrunchy, Jo's Mum couldn't help but shake her head in disapproval. In her mother's eyes, she was dressed like a boy; in Jo's she felt it was what Madonna would wear, if *she* was going to watch an F.A Cup game.

As her overbearing mother reflexively began preening her, and tucking a stray strand of her curly brown hair back behind her ear, Jo's thoughts turned to Andy. No matter what her parents said about him, (and last night they had said plenty), she liked him. She knew of him from her previous school, but in truth everyone in their area knew the family, and by proxy everybody knew Andy. When the local kids played out he was always the first one there, the last to leave, and the one who was always up for mischief. With his close cropped hair, dirty trainers and rogue-ish smile, he looked every inch a little villain. It was an assessment not far from the truth, but he was also lively, funny, fearless, clever and great fun to be with. Andy was old before his time. "Ten years going on twenty six," her Dad had said.

She wondered where he had spent the night, assuming he had not been caught, or driven back by the cold.

"Now be careful," the teenager heard her mother, now finished with her alterations, shout as she slipped into the driver's seat. "I don't like you goin' off to these football games!"

Jo plastered on a fake smile and waved as the car drove past her. Once it rounded the corner, she tucked her jeans back into her hi-tops, and released the strand of hair from behind her ear with an irritated sigh.

"Come 'ead Jo!" her Dad called from down the street as the two men in their near identical black leather jackets continued their walk, "we've gorra grab the 'papers yet!"

Jo shook her head out of her reverie, and jogged to catch up. Despite the hour it seemed like hundreds of people, mainly men and boys, dressed in red, white and yellow scarves and hats were milling around outside the coach depot, or making their way across London Road towards the station. Carrier bags advertising the likes of Wade Smith and Tescos, bulging with thermos flasks, tins of lager, sandwiches and newspapers added further colour to the scene. There was a low level buzz in the air, as Jo dipped and dodged past smile filled conversations about the players, the team or the football in general.

She found Andy outside one of the huge sets of open doors at the back of the station from where the coaches left. He was sitting on the pavement resting against a large street light, the worn knees of his denim jeans tucked under his chin, his arms wrapped tightly around his legs. He looked freezing. His thin nylon, navy Sergio Tacchini track top, wearing even thinner at the elbows, offered little protection against the elements. He reflexively tapped the toes of his grubby, battered, formerly white, Adidas trainers alternately against the curb.

"Come on soft lad," Jo chided, "we'll miss the bus," she said, hurrying past him. Inside however, the vast coach house was packed down one side with a large queue of travelling reds, the dull roar of engines and the thick scent of diesel filled the air. Jo's fears turned towards the possibility that they might not be able to get onto the bus parked at the front of the line.

They took up places behind Jo's father and uncle,

both deep in conversation about Liverpool's possible side for the day.

A man in a dark uniform and bus-man's flat hat waved forward another coach behind the first, and people began to board. The brief knot of tension in Jo's stomach unwound. By ten past seven, they were onboard and on their way to London. A smartly dressed woman in a pastel pink blazer and matching long skirt stood at the front of the bus and, using a microphone, welcomed them aboard. She told them that there was a toilet at the rear, that refreshments were available, and that a video would be shown shortly.

"A toilet!" exclaimed Jo happily, thinking of her queasy stomach.

"A video!" marvelled Andy, his dark eyes lighting up. "Brill! I bet it's Return of the Jedi!!"

"I should've taken that bet," Jo said sarcastically later, as the coach hit the M6 motorway, and with the curtains drawn, the video title "Operation Petticoat" flashed onto the small television screen perched high up at the front of the bus. Andy dug his hands into pockets and pulled a tongue, the young boy feigned annoyance and indifference momentarily, but his gaze quickly drifted back towards the screen.

"Andy?" queried the girl, as soon as she was sure her relatives in the seats in front were firmly engrossed in the movie. "Where did you stay last night?"

"At home."

"What?" Jo exclaimed with real surprise.

"At home," repeated Andy, matter of factly. "How come? Didn't your Mum and Dad find out? Did you sneak in or what?" Questions tumbled out of Jo's jumbled thoughts and Andy noticed she was turning her plastic comb around nervously in her hands.

"No," said Andy, amused. "They let me stay and they've given me the money to go to London. He paused for a moment, before breaking out a conspiratorial grin, "I didn't tell them I'd already paid".

"They let you stay?" Jo mused. "They must love you very much." She began to pull the comb through the underside of her thick, curly hair. "Isn't it against the law or something? My Mum and Dad would have me out like a shot. Aren't yours scared?"

"Nah! They're not bothered," he said dismissively.

"You look shattered," the teenager said, stopping her grooming to look him up and down. "You don't look like you stayed at home," she added sceptically.

Andy cleared his throat and adjusted the zip on his tracksuit top, the navy paint was chipped and the handle had snapped off, meaning he had to pinch the stub awkwardly between his fingers to move it up and down.

"Yeah well, I didn't sleep much. If the wellies had…"

"The wellies?"

"Yeah, y'know the welfare officers? Social workers. They send the bizzies round in the middle of the night if they think you're at home."

"God, that's awful!"

"Ahh, they'd never 'ave got me. I'm not gonna miss this comic mart for anythin'," he said firmly, puffing his chest out.

Jo lapsed into silence. The conversation had left her with a sense of unease, and for a long time, as laughter filled the air around her on the speeding bus, she stared blankly at the television and worried the comb around in her hands. Eventually her mind wandered back to the forthcoming football game, and she began to run through the future goals the reds were going to score, before replacing herself in the fantasy as the goalscorer. She had just decided to add a brilliant individual fourth goal to complete the rout, with a long mazy dribble from her own penalty area when she felt Andy's elbow dig into her ribs.

"I could do that," he announced.

"What?" Jo asked, bewildered, still halfway between the coach and her daydream.

"'Im there, look!" Andy urged, pointing at the television screen. "He's on a submarine and he calls himself a Supply Officer and he robs everything. Cars, trucks, machinery, look he's just stolen a pig! Ah, it's dead funny. He's great. Everyone else calls 'im a scavenger."

"Oh, yeah," said Jo, disinterested.

"Bet if I did that they'd lock me up and throw away the key!"

"I thought they had," Jo smirked.

"Yeah, yeah, dead funny," he retorted, rolling his eyes. "He does it and everyone thinks it's funny, I do it and everyone gets mad."

"It's only a film."

"Yeah, well," Andy said indignantly, "it's not right is all."

"Neither is stealing."

"I've stopped now."

"Oh aye, yeah, now you've been locked up."

"It's not that," he said defensively.

"Well, what is it?"

"I've just stopped that's all," the boy said, shifting his body more towards the window, suggesting he did not want to discuss it further. Feeling backed into a corner, Andy quickly looked to change the subject.

"Where's yer scarf anyway?"
The quick turn of topic threw off Jo's train of thought, and though she had heard the question she still wrinkled her lightly freckled nose and said "wha'?"

"Where. Is. Your. Scarfffff?" Andy played out the word slowly, "Are you goin' deaafff?"

"Oi cheeky!" She retorted with a playful scowl, "I don't wear one, or any 'colours' on aways. It's… well, it keeps you out of trouble. These days…" she paused to remember a warning her father had given her earlier in the season, "… these days you've got to be smart, it doesn't pay to advertise who you support."

"I'll get you one if you want."

"Rob one you mean! I thought you'd given up?"

"I 'ave. Thought i'd scavenge you one tho'"
They both laughed.

"Oh yeah, a right little scavenger you are," Jo smiled warmly and pulled the comb through her hair again. "Anyway," she added, not wanting her lack of colours to be perceived as a lack of allegiance, "I've got loads at home. I just can't wear them, not on aways. Who do you support anyway?"
"Everton," Andy chirped.

"Everton?!" Jo said, with a sneer on her lips.

"Yeah! An' wha'? Better than Liverpool!"

"Go 'way!"

"We are!" And sensing a winning argument added, "We're the Champions!"

"Yeah," Jo sneered again, defiantly, "not for long!"

"Arrr as if!" It was Andy's turn to sneer. "We beat you in the Derby!"

"So?! We beat you at Goodison. Anyway, you don't even go the game!"

"I do!" He said defiantly.

"When?" Jo challenged sceptically.

"Sometimes."

"Oh yeah?" Jo pushed at his uncertainty.

"I do too! I used to go all the time. I used to LOVE going," Andy explained. "We used to cadge the money. It was great!"

"Cadge the money?"

"Yeah, y'know '*lends 10p to get in mate*'" Andy mimicked himself, with an even more exaggerated accent. "I used to get enough for the game AND have a couple of quid over."

"You're joking!"

"Honest," Andy said seriously. "I haven't been for a while though. Am not always allowed at weekends, though they've taken us a couple of times. I saw your lot the other week, against Oxford. Terrible."
"Terrible!" Jo blurted out. "We won 6-0!!!"

"Yeah I know, terrible," he said with a wink. They both laughed again.

"Anyway, if you're that keen why aren't you going to see Everton today?"

"I've told you. I've got to go to the Comic Mart."

"Probably for the best, they'll get beat anyway."

"No they won't."

"They will."

"They won't, Liverpool will though."

"They won't!"

"They will."

"I'll murder you in a minute!" Jo cracked under the strain.

"Oh yeah, you and whose Army?" Andy taunted.

Jo laughed, as the rest of the coach, seeing the motorway signs for London, broke out into song. She held aloft her imaginary scarf and sang in his face…

"We're on the march with Kenny's army, WE'RE ALL GOING TO WEM-BER-LEEEE!"

Andy grinned and with feigned indignance sunk into his seat as the raucous Reds-packed coach streaked on.

CHAPTER THREE:

SPORT WITH STAMPS

Saturday. 5th April 1986. 11:25am.

  Andy had thought that Liverpool's Skelhorne Street Bus Station was big, but Victoria Station was HUGE by comparison. He stood there, mouth open in awe of the scale of his surroundings.
  So many buses. So many people scurrying around, suitcases in hand. Some even had cases on wheels, like his mother's shopping trolly, pulling them along behind them. Others, millions of them it seemed, queued at gates or used the lines of payphones or looked lost, or stood around. Millions of people in different shapes and sizes, old and young, black and white and every shade and variation in between. Bright sportswear, sensible suits, a mass of humanity and a cacophony of noise.
  Andy heard many different accents and languages and marvelled at how such obvious foreigners to London could look so at home. He had never felt so out of place. Nor had he ever felt so small, lost in a sea of hustling legs.
  "Don't forget, two o'clock," he heard Jo's dad say to her, "don't be late, and don't," - at this he turned to look at Andy -

"don't get up to any mischief. And that goes for you double sunshine," he said, poking a finger at the boy.

As the two brothers, near twins with their thick dark hair, moustaches, black leather jackets and white adidas trainers, disappeared into the crowd, Jo pulled an overly sour face behind them. Her companion laughed.

"Come on, let's get outta this crowd," she instructed. Outside however was no less busy. People spilled in all directions, cars packed the streets, the cool air filled with the sounds of motor engines and the occasional car horn. The people reminded Andy of the ants that had poured out from under a flagstone in his street after he had put a banger under it last bonfire night. Only the mass of vibrant colours was different. "Ants don't wear clothes," he said out loud without meaning to.

"You what?" Jo asked with a raised eyebrow. "Ants don't wear clothes? Well, I never knew that!"

Andy laughed with embarrassment and tried to explain. "If a spaceship looked down on all these people, they'd all look like ants…"

"Don't start with flying saucers again, space kid."

"Only the clothes," continued Andy, determined to dig himself out of a hole, "would show them that it was people. They would have to fly pretty low to see that though."

"Maybe that's why they are spotted all the time. They're flying low to see what the latest fashions are," Jo said smiling, and holding the bright purple hem of her jacket, did an exaggerated walk and pirouette whilst looking up at the sky.

"Very funny." He looked around. "Where are we anyway?"

"Victoria."

"Yeah, alright smart aleck, but where's that?" And with that he pulled out a dog eared magazine that had been wedged in the lining under his jacket, and proceeded to leaf through the pages.

"Here it is," he announced presently and, pushing the book towards his companion, gave it to her and pointed to an advert in the bottom corner of the page. The full page ad was in black and white and announced in large letters:

> COMIC MART. Britain's largest fantasy fan gathering
> At the Central Hall, Westminster, London.

Another heading said:

> HOW TO GET THERE

And beneath that was a map with a large arrow pointing to the hall and information about the underground and the buses. The advert concluded with the information:

> FREE - DOORS OPEN MID-DAY

"It'll be quicker by tube," said Jo, feeling the seasoned traveller compared to her young friend who she knew had never been out of Liverpool before, save for trips to the coast, Southport and Rhyl.

As it turned out, she could not have been more right. They discovered that the station they wanted; St. James Park, was only one stop from Victoria, and though they missed this stop and had to get off at the next one, Westminster, they were soon staring up at the huge dome of Central Hall.

"Is that it, d'ye think?" Jo asked, looking at the ornate stone wreath carving above the main entrance in awe. "In there?"

"I think so. Let's walk around the back and see if there are any signs," Andy suggested.

They spotted two androgynous teenagers in heavy black eye makeup walking ahead of them, and as they got closer the youngsters could hear them talking about someone called "the Dark Knight".

"They're going to the Mart," said Andy, barely able to contain his excitement. "That's Batman they're talking about! Frank Miller's doing a new version, it might even be on sale today!"

It was all gobbledegook to Jo, but she watched the two youths, with their languid gait and ripped black jeans, as they entered the Hall by one of the two rear entrances.

"We'll follow them," said Andy. "They'll know the way."

As he spoke, the sky which had been darkening ominously throughout their short walk finally decided it could shoulder its burden no more, and started to deposit its rain heavily onto the heads of Jo and Andy. The colour of the pavement deepened and the rain bounced high around their ankles as they dashed headlong for the doors, past another teen in black, and crashed through them, laughing loudly.

Inside, Jo stood looking at her feet, shaking off the rain that had beaded on the surface of her polyester tracksuit jacket.

"They've gone," Andy's voice caused her to raise her head.

"Who? Oh, yeah, that was quick wasn' it?" She looked

around, puzzled. "Where'd they go?"

"Dunno," the boy shrugged, the navy shoulders of his jacket darkened already as the rain soaked in. "What's that?" he said, scrunching up his face as he strained to hear.

"What's what?"

"That noise, it sounds like… Hymns?!" Jo, a sceptical look etched into her face, strained to listen.

"Hymns? Oh aye, yeah it does doesn't it? But it's Saturday isn' it? Yeah it's Saturday. No-one sings hymns on a Saturday… Err… Do they?" Jo added, uncertainly.

"Maybe they're practising."

"Oh yeah, that's it," Jo said, pleased to have the mystery cleared up.

"It's coming from down there," Andy pointed, "so the Mart must be upstairs. Come on."

As they approached the staircase the singing stopped and was replaced by the chanting rhythm of a church congregation saying communal prayers. The youngsters looked at each other, baffled as to why a church service should be taking place on a Saturday. They shrugged their shoulders, pulled faces that said "beats me!" and carried on up the stairs, but Jo's steps were more considered now.

"Maybe it's a Jewish service," she suggested as they reached the landing. "It's not half-quiet up here. Where is everyone? I thought you said collecting comics was dead popular."

"It is," he replied defensively.

"Well it looks about as popular as the number 12 shirt in a Cup Final to me."

"Come on, let's have a look in here," urged Andy unperturbed, pushing his way through a set of doors.

Inside they found a large room full of objects hidden under white sheets. Dust motes danced in the air, churned up by their arrival.

"Andy, let's get out of here," said Jo nervously and half turned back towards the door.

"Hang about," Andy headed for the nearest sheeted object which stood a full two heads taller than him, and promptly disappeared underneath it.

"Andy! Get out of there! Come on Andy!" Jo hissed as loudly as she dared, tentatively stepping further into the room towards her young friend's feet which protruded from under the sheet along with four wooden legs. Grabbing a corner of the material, Jo pulled it up above her head.

Andy stood with his back to her, his nose pressed up against a sheet of glass.

"That's better, keep that sheet there, I can see now. Eh look! They're cases like they have in the museum."

"Since when have YOU been in the museum?"

"Loads of times," the boy announced, but seeing his companion's doubtful look, added, "especially when it's raining."

Jo moved closer and flung the sheet with a whoosh over the top of the display case. "Stamps?" she said with a puzzled tone.

"Stamps." Agreed Andy.

"Not comics?"

"Stamps."

"From... Finland," Jo read from the small cards in the exhibition cabinet.

"And Russia!" Shouted Andy from the next cabinet.

"Andy!" Jo whispered loudly as she saw her friend dashing noisily from one display to another, throwing back their covers and broadcasting the nationality of the stamps in each case.

"And the USA."

"Stop it!"

"And Canada."

"Stop it you!" Jo hissed.

"And France. And…" As he tried to push past Jo to get to another cabinet she grabbed him. Andy giggled and panted from his exertion. Jo pulled him up by his jacket until they were face to face, nose to nose.

Through gritted teeth she asked venomously, "I thought you said this was a Comic Mart!" Her rage was barely concealed.

"It is."

"Oh yeah? It's a stamp exhibition. A… a *sporting* stamp exhibition! Stamps. All. About. Sport." Her voice was quiet but then she shouted, "AND IT'S NOT EVEN OPEN!!" and flung the boy down roughly to the ground.

While she rubbed her hands together as if to remove a layer of dirt or dust, Andy rummaged frantically inside his jacket and flicked through the pages of his magazine.

"Look, look!" He urged. "Comic Mart. Look. April 5th, 1986. Look. Twelve Noon. It is! Look!"

Jo looked, her rage simmering behind a straight face. "Well," she said slowly, "where is it then, smart lad?"

"It must be… err… somewhere else."

"No kidding. You really are a clever one aren't yer? Somewhere else… OF COURSE IT'S SOMEWHERE ELSE!"

Andy pulled a hurt face and, turning, ran to the doors and rushed out.

"Ey!!! What about these covers?!" she shouted after

him. Jo stood, looking down the room- all the cases were uncovered, and several sheets lay sprawled across the wooden floor- turned and walked out. "The little villain," she muttered to herself as she closed the door on the devastation.

Outside she saw Andy along the corridor at another set of doors, and watched him disappear inside as she walked towards him.

There were several windows dotted around the corridor and hazy sunshine shone in wide rays that seemed to shimmer and dance with speckles of dust as they fell across her path. This made the darkness Jo found in the room beyond the next doors all the more blinding. As the heavy wooden door shut behind her with a thud, she found herself completely enveloped in impenetrable gloom.

"Andy!" She wanted to shout out but the quietness around her made her whisper. Nevertheless it was probably the loudest whisper she could manage, and clearly betrayed her quickly returning anger.

"Stop messin' about Andy! I don't want to play hide and bloody seek. I'm leaving... Andy? Andy!"

She heard a noise to her right, but as she turned towards it, another louder sound pulled her back to her original position. The second sound was directly in front of her, though some distance away. Jo took a step forward and a hand suddenly clamped over her mouth from behind. An arm grabbed her around the neck and pulled her backwards. She tensed instinctively and though panic flooded her brain she knew it wasn't Andy. This person was bigger. She tried to scream, but the hand was locked firm...

THE MAN WHO STOLE THE WORLD CUP

COMIC MART

BRITAIN'S LARGEST FANTASY FAN GATHERING AT THE CENTRAL HALL, WESTMINSTER, LONDON.

COMIC MART

THE PLACE TO GET FILM MAGAZINES, BOOKS POSTERS; COMIC BOOKS (MARVEL, D.C., ETC.), POSTERS, ART PORTFOLIOS, BADGES, FANZINES, SCIENCE FICTION/FANTASY MATERIAL AND ANYTHING ELSE YOU'VE EVER WANTED TO COLLECT! OVER 100 STALLS OF FANTASY PARAPHERNALIA TO MAKE YOUR MIND BOGGLE!

FUTURE MARTS

AUGUST 2ND 1986
OCTOBER 11TH 1986

DEALERS:

FOR INFORMATION PLEASE SEND AN S.A.E. TO:—

TITAN DISTRIBUTORS,
P.O. BOX 250,
LONDON E3 4RT
ENGLAND.

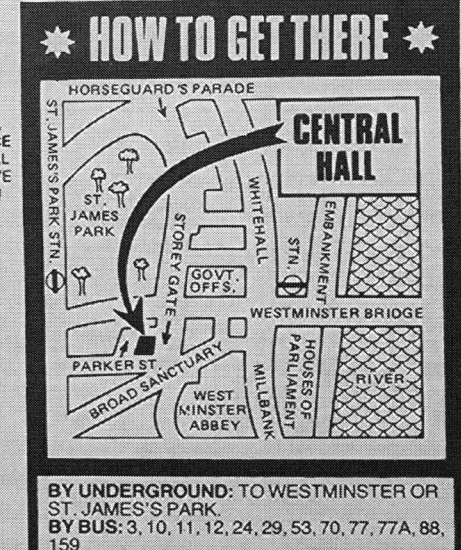

HOW TO GET THERE

BY UNDERGROUND: TO WESTMINSTER OR ST. JAMES'S PARK.
BY BUS: 3, 10, 11, 12, 24, 29, 53, 70, 77, 77A, 88, 159

FREE — DOORS OPEN MID-DAY

CHAPTER FOUR:

THE MAN IN BLACK

Sunday. 20th March 1966. 10:55am

Most of Jo's dreams and practically all of her daydreams concerned her footballing prowess and how she would put it to use winning trophies for Liverpool Football Club, and occasionally even for England. She enjoyed these fantasies immensely.

None of her other daydreams gave her as much pleasure but they all gave her some enjoyment or satisfaction in their own way.

Even in her least favourite make-believe (the one drilled into by her mother every time she left the house), where she was attacked from behind by an unknown assailant, she always enjoyed the way her mind stayed clear; always revelled in the way she stamped on her attacker's toes, spun around, kneed him viciously, pushed her fingers in his eyes, and karate chopped him to the ground. She'd seen Karate Kid three times at the pictures, and always marvelled at the certainty of her response to such situations.

Now with a hand cutting off her voice and a forearm

cutting off her breath in a pitch black, musty room, she froze. Her brain raced, her blood turned to ice and her limbs stiffened. She was petrified.

Jo felt herself being pulled backwards and could do nothing. Terror transfixed her. Irrationally she thought of her mother's smug "I told you so" face, and how much her Dad would shout when she was late meeting up.

They stopped. The noise Jo had heard ahead in the distance sounded again, then suddenly a shaft of light pierced the gloom as a door was opened some yards away in the darkness.

Her attacker stopped and clamped his hand tighter on her mouth. The smell of leather gloves filled her nostrils. He seemed to hold his breath and Jo thought she could feel his heart pounding against her back. It mirrored her own.

Through widened eyes, Jo saw two figures silhouetted in the light of the doorway.

"I fought it'd be 'eavier," came a thick Cockney accent in the blackness. "You'd 'ardly fink it was werf anyfink at all it's so light."

"Never mind the weight, it's worth its weight in gold, literally. Let's just get it out of here." Another, more cultured voice answered.

Still gripped firm, Jo watched as the figures moved out of the light to be replaced by clear footsteps moving ever closer in the shadows.

She became aware of her captor again and felt the fear rise in her stomach. Her attacker seemed uncertain but Jo was still frozen like a statue, unable to move. Suddenly she felt a pressure behind her knees and she buckled and fell forward. The unknown assailant gripped tightly and ensured that the teenager was lowered gently to the floor with hardly a sound. She felt herself being pulled to the right so that she was curled up on her side like a ball.

Hot breath, sweet and pleasant, played across her cheek as a soft, agreeable voice whispered in her ear. "Please, keep quiet. I beg you."

Whether this request had the desired result is impossible to say, as Jo's limbs were still numb and refused to respond. Her attacker released their grip, leaving Jo prone on the ground.

In the darkness she heard the footsteps move closer, echoing in the emptiness around her, but barely audible over the sound of her own pulse, pounding in her ears.

Where was Andy?? What had been done to him? He would never willingly be this quiet. Heaven knew he had always been capable of looking after himself, had always had to it seemed, but she was much older. Jo felt responsible. She had to do something.

Taking a deep breath she tested her newly found motivation and raised herself onto her elbow. From there she moved to her knees, felt forward and found the support of a glass case that stood over her. Carefully she pulled herself to her feet.

Her brain was working again. She moved deliberately around the glass cabinet to its opposite side, nearer the unknown voices but away from where her attacker had left her. Trying desperately to calm her pounding heart and rasping breath, she surveyed the scene with eyes finally acquainted with the dark.

The footsteps moved ever closer. They seemed to come from one side of the shaft of light that stabbed into the gloom

36

like a sword. This impression was confirmed when one of the figures swayed back into illumination at its far edge.

At that moment a figure in black dashed across the bright wedge of yellow and bundled the two men to the ground, grabbed at something held in the arms of one of them, and started running back along the light towards Jo, carrying the bundle like a rugby ball clutched to his chest.

Jo only knew that this man was her assailant, the one who had done something to Andy and terrified the life out of her. A fire ignited in the pit of her stomach. He would not escape, whoever he was, or whatever his game was. She wouldn't let him. Rugby wasn't Jo's cup of tea, but on the football pitch she'd taken out lads twice her size for years.

As the man in black drew level with her position Jo, channeling her inner Graeme Souness, executed a textbook sliding tackle at his feet, throwing in her hip for extra force, and sending him crashing to the cold, stone floor. "Ooofff!" he exclaimed daintily as air slammed out of his lungs.

The man clung desperately to his prized package as he tumbled over but moaned in despair when some part of it flew back over his head and bounced, with loud clumps, back down the room. It came to rest at the feet of the other two men, who were noisily picking themselves up.

"It's the guards!"

"I *fought* you said there weren't any guards on a Sunday," the cockney remarked.

"Never mind that, let's get out of here."

"'Ere, I've got somefing."

"Grab it and run," came the reply and in a flurry of noise and movement the two figures raced towards Jo and the man in black, leapt over their prostate bodies and crashed out of the doors that Jo had originally entered through. That seemed an eternity ago, in reality little more than a minute had passed.

The person beside her moaned. *'Surely i've not hurt him that much,'* thought Jo. *'I'd better get out of here!'* She raised herself to her knees and then stopped, her thoughts flashing back to her missing friend.

"Where's Andy, you?!" she barked as threateningly as she could. Adrenaline rushed through her veins, giving her unexpected courage.

"Andy?" The soft voice seemed to melt Jo's fear. The man seemed dazed. "Oh, the boy. He's alright. I had time to get him out of this. You were too much of a surprise."

The voice was all wrong but Jo couldn't think clearly enough to understand the discrepancy.

"What have you done to him?" Jo demanded.

"Done? Nothing." And sensing the teenager's uncertainty, "Honestly… I'll take you to him… the time's gone here."

The black clad figure rose elegantly to their feet. "This way."

Jo followed back towards the doorway and then to the left just before they reached the door. She expected to see Andy's body on the floor but even in the gloom she knew there was nothing. No sign of him.

"Give me your hand."

Not surprisingly Jo hesitated. This man had just attacked her, but there was a disarming warmth to his voice.

"I understand your fear, but I can't take you to your friend unless you hold my hand."

Jo still hung back, wrinkling her freckled nose in disapproval. "What is this?"

"Okay look," the stranger said, clearly exasperated. "Just hold my sleeve."

Jo hesitated again then did as she was told. The voice belied the threat she felt.

The material of the coat sleeve was cool and smooth. As was the transition.

She heard a faint, digital chirping noise. At one moment Jo was in the darkened room filled with covered display cabinets and memories of recent terror, the next she was in a brightly lit cavern of a room, lined on all sides with books beneath a vaulted ceiling.

In the middle of the room was a highly-polished, circular, wooden table and sat on the floor next to it, legs crossed, reading a book, was Andy.

CHAPTER FIVE:

THE JULES RIMET TROPHY

<u>Limbo. Time and Date Unknown.</u>

    Jo should have been startled by the sudden change of environment, should have questioned her whereabouts, but the sight of Andy, fit and well, filled her thoughts to the exclusion of all else.

    However, her relief soon turned to anger as she thought of all that worry she'd had over him, for nothing. Not only was he not hurt, wounded or dead in a ditch, but in fact he looked perfectly, infuriatingly contented, sitting in the middle of this strange room. All thoughts of the stranger vanished as a fury rose up inside her and spewed out.

    "ANDY!!! WHERE HAVE YOU BEEN?! I'VE BEEN WORRIED SICK ABOUT YOU, YOU LITTLE IDIOT! I've been attacked, choked, thrown around in the dark, scared half to death, and all that time, ALL THAT TIME, you've been sitting here like some… some BLOODY GARDEN GNOME! Look at you," she said, stabbing an
accusing finger towards him, "reading books whilst i'm fighting for my life! I could've been killed! Not that you care!

Ohhh no! All YOU think about's your bloody Comic Mart. Well, that's it," she continued, raising her accusing finger to the wooden beamed ceiling to mark her point, "I'm going."

She spun on her heel, and stamped her foot like an infantry soldier about to set off on a march. "Come on then, chop chop."

She waited a moment, the look of steely determination on her face quickly flashed with anger when her command was not followed by the sound of Andy scrambling to his feet in compliance.

"Can't," he said.
Jo huffed indignantly.

"Well, i'll go on my own then, don't come crying to me when you're lost forev… What d'ye mean 'can't?'"

"Can't. I've tried all the doors. They're all locked, even I can't open them."

"What about the door we came in…" Jo turned as she spoke, and finally taking in her environment, her mouth fell open. Behind her, where a door should have been, was only an old fashioned fireplace, encased with book shelves, and a green leather, wingback chair. Her head reflexively swivelled to take in more of the room. The longest sides, to her left and right both had bookshelves that ran at least ten feet high, with each broken up what appeared to be two dark green metal filing cabinets each with another couple of shelves between them. Past the dark wooden table, the surface of which shimmered with a faint, mysterious glow, were two waist height 'L-shaped" wooden sideboards, framed with the same polished dark wood as the table, with a pale green, golden and burgundy flowered wallpaper inset. These sat either side of a clear path of green and wine red patterned persian rug which lead to the only door in the room. It too was made of a rich, mahogany wood, the grain just visible through the stain and polish. It was also too far away to have possibly been Jo's point of entry.

"But, but…" Jo stammered. "… that's…" She turned to face Andy who had put down his book and was walking towards her.

"Impossible?" he helped. He watched the anger rise like a thundercloud in her face as she turned her attention finally to the Man in Black.

The mystery man stood a few yards away to Jo's left and, unaware of the girl's attention, was giving his to a detailed examination of the gold object he held in his hands. The harsh overhead lighting reflected brightly from it's shaped surface, and the man recoiled visibly at the glare. "Light setting Fedora Three please MIKE" he said softly, and with an affirmative sounded digital 'chirrup', the overhead lighting dimmed and half a dozen beautiful stained glass lamps around the room illuminated in unison. It gave the room a much more welcoming, cosy vibe, Jo thought, but it was insufficient to quell her anger.

"What have you done with it?!" Jo shouted, and when this failed to attract his attention away from his find, added, "Ey, you!"

As if coming out of a trance the man looked up and turned to face the two youngsters. He appeared to be in his late thirties, stood about five feet nine, and was of slim build. Jo noticed he had thin lips, dark eyes and black hair brushed back flat with grease. A pale scar stood out on his cheek against his sallow complexion. He was wearing a ribbed, black, polo necked jumper beneath a black, shiny two piece suit.

Jo used her best stern voice and demanded, "What have you done with the door?"

"The door? Oh that's still there, you just can't see it." Again, the voice was all wrong; it just didn't fit the man they saw before them.

"Are you mad mate?" She said, her nose wrinkling and eyes squinting as her tone turned to a sneer. "We just wanna go. What's this all about?"

"What this is all about- is this," replied the man, holding up the gold statuette, "and unfortunately I can't allow you to leave until I've had time to assess what your untimely arrival means."

Jo's eyes alighted on the statuette. It looked very familiar. It was gold coloured on a black base, about twelve inches tall and was shaped like a woman with wings. Realisation came in a flash and she felt a shiver run down her spine. Her stomach lurched like she had just been driven over a humped back bridge at speed. In her mind's eye she could see this object, this prize clearly in the pages of a book she had sat on her bedside table at home.

"Can I see?" she asked, holding out her hands tentatively.

"Yes of course." The stranger held it out for her.

Taking a step forward, the teenager, with a nylon rustle of her open jacket, nimbly grabbed the trophy and stepped back out of reach with a skip.

She looked closely at the gleaming golden object. The cockney fella back in the darkened room had been right, it was very light. It couldn't have weighed more than a few pounds. *Worth it's weight in gold,* she remembered.

"Andy?" Jo whispered out of the corner of her mouth.

The boy, who had been quietly studying the books around the fireplace that should have been a door, moved to her side.

"Wha'?" He squinted at the writing. "What does 'coupe du monde' mean?" he asked, struggling over the foreign words.

"It's…" Jo gulped, her voice took on a reverential tone, "The World Cup." She let the enormity of those three words hang in the air.

"The wha'? You're kidding!?"

"I'm not. It's the World Cup. It has to be. Look at the plaques on the side. See? Brazil 1962. Brazil 1958. It's the bloody Jules Rimet trophy! It says it right here at the bottom. Uruguay 1930. Italy 1934. Look. I read all about it in a book I got for Christmas. But, what's it doing here?"

"Ey yeah, you're right. It should be in Mexico for the World Cup in the Summer."

"No soft lad!" Jo said in exasperation. "It should be in Brazil."

"Brazil?"

"Yeah, after they won it for the third time in 1970 they got to keep it. They play for a completely different trophy now."

"Oh aye?"

"Yeah of course! You always keep a cup if you win it three times, well unless they change it halfway through like they did when the Reds won the League Cup four times, and they changed it to the stupid Milk Cup."

"So it's the *old* World Cup then?" Andy brought Jo back to the point. "And this fella's robbed it?" He turned to the man in question with a nod of approval.

"We won't tell mate, honest," Andy announced. "Just give us a few quid and we'll be off. Our little secret." He made a locking motion in front of his closed mouth and gave a conspiratorial wink for good measure.

"Andy!" Shouted Jo. "We don't want anything off this… this.. person. We're not thieves… ARE WE?" It wasn't a question.

"Err," Andy hesitated only long enough to see Jo's face. "Yeah, no, we're not thieves, course not." He said, changing his posture like an actor who'd just remembered their lines.

"1970 you said?" The stranger questioned and began to pace nervously up and down.

"Yeah, in Mexico."

"Brazil won the Cup in Mexico in 1970? That's what you are saying? This cup?"

"Yeah," she reiterated.

"What year is this?"

"What?"

"What year is this? What year are we in now?" the man asked, as casually as one would asking the time of day.

"1986. What's that got to do with it? Look, what is all this?"

The stranger sighed deeply. "Have a closer look at the trophy. How many plates are there?"

Jo did as she was told, albeit with a bemused look on her face. "Seven".

"And how many should there be?"

"Nine. Two are missing."

"Fast math," Andy chimed in cheekily.

"Shut up Andy," Jo hissed.

"Which ones?"

"The last two, England and Brazil."

"England?" The stranger cheered up visibly.

"So England won the World Cup. Then I have been successful. This is great news!"

"All these books are about football," Andy muttered, to no-one in particular.

"What d'yer mean, successful? Where are the missing plates, and what's this even doing here? Is it supposed to be on display here? I've not heard about it."

"But how could you, you're not supposed to be here. Hmm, nineteen eighty six?" He mused.

"Look mister," Jo started to say, "you're right, we…

"Mister?" the stranger interrupted with a bemused smile. "Oh, of course," he laughed. "I had completely forgotten!" And so saying his hands went to his head and pulled at the greased, black hair. It came away in his hands, revealing a hair net. Once removed, this in turn revealed a shock of blonde. The Man in Black shook his head and ran his fingers through his bob-length, lightly curled, blonde hair.

"I'll never get a comb through this," the pleasant voice said, and blew a loose strand away from his grizzled face. Jo and Andy looked on, first in horror, then in growing gory fascination as his slender hands pulled at the face beneath the hair, removing bits of skin, lips, the scar and even the nose and ears.

When he had finished, the delicate features of a young woman in her mid twenties looked back at them. The Man in Black was now a… Woman in Black.

"You're a… Bird?" Andy blurted out, and received an immediate punch to the arm from Jo.
"The term you're looking for is 'Woman' you little pig. You are, aren't you?" She checked, cautiously.

"Yes, I suppose I am," she said with a sparkle in her

eyes. "My name is Fedora. And I must go and shower. Make yourselves at home Andy and…?"

"Jo."

"Jo. Right," she replied, as though confirming a fact she had already suspected. Then, before either of the youngsters had overcome their surprise Fedora picked up the Jules Rimet Trophy and strode to the doorway to the right of them. She waved her left wrist in front of it, and the audible sound of a locking mechanism could be heard. She pulled open the heavy wooden door and left.

Andy moved first. He bolted over to the door and tried the handle.

"Locked again," he announced with a frown.

"He's a woman," said Jo, dazed.

"She's crackers," said Andy. "I didn't understand anything she said, did you?"

"No, not really. That's defo the World Cup though, the one that was…"

"Was what?"

"Stolen..." Jo said, with a puzzled expression. "It was stolen in 1966." She struggled to remember. "I read about it. Some dog found it a week later."

"So?"

"Nothing," she said, unable to shake the feeling that she was missing something.

Andy returned to look at the books inset into the walls, and Jo joined him.

"You know, you were right," she said. "They really are all about football. Gosh. He - I mean, SHE's, well, she's got everything. Books about different teams, different competitions, different years, different players."

The library, as it were, was far from complete. Though to Jo's mind it was likely the single largest collection of football books in the world, many of the shelves were half filled, and some were bare. To either side of her were the tall green filing cabinets she'd noticed earlier. Each had three deep drawers, with ascending letters of the alphabet hand written on browning paper in the top left corner of each. Jo scanned down them and found "J-M on the bottom drawer. She slid it open. And kept sliding it open. Jo gave it a frown. The drawer was impossibly deep, too deep. She stood up and looked at the top of the unit. From front to back it was a foot and a half at best. She shook her head and pulled at the drawer again until the letter "L" appeared atop a brown cardboard divider. She quickly flicked through until she found a file marked 'Liverpool F.C.'. She sifted lightly through it's contents, largely consisting of old copies of the Daily Mirror and the Liverpool Post and Echo. Headlines flicked past of the club's early days, Liverpool promoted from the Second Division, Liverpool win the FA Cup. Jo smiled, she loved all the old stories about the Reds, but what she saw next made her blood run cold.

LIVERPOOL FOOTBALL CLUB DISBANDED.

"What the hell?" Jo said, the hairs on the back of her neck standing on end. She read on:
"Sad day for the city as the Red's close their doors for the final time" read the sub heading.
"Liverpool chairman Eric Roberts today formerly ceased trading operations for Liverpool Football Club, Anfield stadium and all of the club's subsidiaries. "This decision does

not come lightly…" In a panic, Jo scanned further down the page and her eyes fell upon a familiar name. "Visibly distressed, Liverpool boss Bill Shankly, speaking to the Echo's football correspondent, said 'it is a dark day for the players, the staff, the city and it's people. We set out to conquer the world, but it seems the world did not wish to be conquered.' Liverpool become the third side this week to follow suit following the collapse of the Football League structure.."

Jo pushed the paper away, and sat back on the floor in shock; her brain unable to process the new information.

"Disbanded?" She muttered.

"This lock's weird, it's got these little lights by it. If you've got a pair of scissors or something I could try pickin' it," Andy interrupted, shocking Jo back to reality. She stood up, shook her head, and pushed the cabinet draw shut with her right instep.

"You'll do no such thing, you little villain," she snapped, but on second thoughts added, "D'yer think you could?"

Something about this place didn't add up. She walked over to the door, and sure enough, around the brass barrel of the branded "YALE" lock, were maybe a dozen tiny blinking lights, connected by a network of fine, silver threads, like cobwebs but less organic, and more technical. It reminded Jo of the circuit board inside her school calculator, but much more intricate.

"It's worth a try, have you got anythin' that might work?" He looked at the dark curls tied back atop her head. "A bobby pin or somethin'?"

"A bobby pin?! Hahaha! It's 1986, not 1955! There must be a way out though. How did we get in?"

"I was just thrown in," Andy explained. "I went into the room. It was dark. I put my hand out to find the light switch. Something grabbed my arm and swung me round and *whoosh*, here I was. I searched all over but couldn't find the door I'd come in by, or the person who'd lashed me in. Every corner, every wall. Nothing." Andy paused. "I gave up in the end."

Jo related what had happened to her in the room and concluded, "I held onto her sleeve and here I am."

They decided to search the shelves again to see if they could find a hidden switch. All Jo found were more football books, artefacts and periodicals, normally she would've been in her element, but she remained haunted by the words of a broken Bill Shankly.

She'd been a baby when he left the club in 1974, but her Dad and Uncle always spoke about the former Liverpool boss with such reverence, forever quoting his best lines. Jo pretty much knew his powerful "Bastion of Invincibility" speech from the steps of St. Georges Hall by heart before she knew her ABC's. When the news broke of his passing in 1981, it was treated almost like a death in the family. The man was supposed to be a towering pillar of strength, not a broken, sad old man.

After a time Jo broke the silence. "Andy?"

"Yeah?"

"I'm scared."

"You're not," Andy said- his attention once again back on the anachronistic door lock.

"I am," Jo insisted forcefully.

"Give over!"

"I am," she insisted again.

"Well I'm not," Andy boasted.

"You liar."

"I'm not! Well, I might be a liar, but I'm not scared!"

"Who d'yer think you're kiddin'??" You're scared soft you are!"

"Am not," Andy declared, stepping towards her pushing his fists to his hips and puffing out his chest. "You are!"

"Urgh! Impossible! We're in a locked room, with mad books that shouldn't exist, being held captive by a fella who's actually a bird…"

"Woman," Andy chirped in.

Jo reflexively ground her teeth. "A woman who has the stolen World Cup trophy and is named after a bloody hat!! If you're not scared it's not 'cause you're brave, it's because you're an idiot!"

"There's no need for anyone to feel scared. I have no intention of harming you." Fedora's calm voice from the doorway startled them.

"Then let us out of here!" Jo demanded.

"Yeah!" Andy chipped in. "You better had, or else!" The woman smiled with a disarming warmth. "I'd better explain. Come and sit down kids."

"We're not kids," said Andy belligerently.

"Well you look like kids to me," said Fedora.

"Well a minute ago you looked like a man to me, so don't give us a lecture on what we are or aren't!"

The older woman paused for a moment to reflect on his comment, before nodding to herself.

"Fair enough. Now, this way please my young friends. All will become clear."

JOHN. J MACHIN

CHAPTER SIX:

THE TEN BOB NOTE

Limbo. Time and Date Unknown.

"Welcome to Limbo," Fedora said as they took chairs around the circular centre table. Similarly to the door it looked like an object from two eras. It was made from rich mahogany wood, ornately trimmed, but its polished surface was laced with veins of silver circuitry interspersed with myriad blinking lights.

"Limbo?! We're not dead are we?" asked Jo in a panic, her catholic upbringing flooding her brain.

Fedora laughed. "No Jo, you're not dead, that's just what I call this place because, well, it's neither here nor there," she said, as though the words actually made sense. "It's between one place and another - one time and another. Actually, technically ALL times and all others, but i'm getting rather metaphysical," she chuckled lightly to herself.

"I bloody told you she was crackers!" Said Andy to her friend, his face scrunched up in disdain.

Fedora laughed again. "I know it's hard to believe and a bit complicated, but i'll try to explain."

Despite their current pseudo-hostage situation, her playful tone and friendly demeanour had taken the edge from Jo and Andy's emotions. In spite of the insanity of the situation, both found their curiosities piqued. Fedora began her story with a sentence that made perfect sense and no sense at all…

"I'm from the future," she stated. "And I have used this," she spread her arms wide to indicate the room around her and beyond. "And this" she said, and pointed to a bracelet on her left wrist. At a glance the golden adornment looked very much like a nice piece of jewellery, not everyday jewellery, more the kind that Jo's grandmother would keep in a box on her dressing table, for special occasions, the kind of special occasions that women owned jewellery for, but never actually attended. The kind of jewellery that you'd get shouted at for borrowing and taking to a school disco. Its ornate design, and the tarnish on the gold finish gave it a lived in quality that meant it looked fairly unremarkable at a glance, but look closer and the more fascinating it became. On closer inspection, the metal itself seemed to constantly shift it's hue, not changing its colour so much as the shade of gold. Jo found herself mesmerised by the shifting and rippling patterns, almost as though it had a life of its own, so lost was she in its rhythm, she almost lost track of Fedora's story.

"This I use to bring me backwards in time."

"To nineteen eighty six," said Jo, almost absent mindedly.

"No. To nineteen SIXTY-six."

"YEEEERRRSE!" Andy shouted, shaking Jo from her reverie.

"What?"

"I KNEW IT!" he continued, almost shaking with excitement.

"What are you blithering about?" Jo snapped.

"TIME TRAVEL!"

"Time travel?"

"TIME TRAVEL!"

"Time? Travel? You're as daft as she is," screeched Jo, losing patience and letting her nerves get the better of her again. She shot up from her chair, sending it squealing backwards across pale wooden floor boards. "Don't encourage her, she's probably just an escaped loony! And YOU," she pointed at Fedora, "with your mad books and weird nana-jewellery, don't encourage him, filling his little brain with this science-fiction nonsense!"

"Jo, listen," said Fedora softly, with obvious concern. "Those plaques on the trophy? The ones you thought were missing?"

"Yeah, what of it?"

"Those plates aren't 'missing', those tournaments haven't been played yet. What happened in that room earlier, with those men, took place before the 1966 World Cup Final.

"It's like Doctor 'oo," said Andy, with wide eyes and beaming smile.

"That's just daft," Jo declared. "We. Us? Yeah?" she gestured at the three of them. "We are in nineteen EIGHTY six, we are in Central Hall for his stupid comics, the Reds are playing in the Cup today AND…" she stabbed a finger toward Fedora, " Doctor WHO, is a man, even I know that you fool!"

"Well, actually…" Fedora began to interrupt, but thought better of it, "no nevermind."

The threesome remained there in silence for a moment,

the sound of Jo's agitated breathing, and a low electronic hum from the table between them only serving to underscore the standoff.

"Look," Fedora said, "I don't suppose any amount of reasoning from me will persuade you. The only thing to do is to take you outside and let you see for yourselves."

"OKAY!!" Andy blurted out excitedly. Time travel was his number one greatest sci-fi love, well, that and talking computers, and though the street kid cynic in him was telling him that it must all be a giant prank, his inner geek was about ready to explode at the possibilities.

Fedora turned to Jo, who was a little less enthusiastic.
"Sure." she said flatly.

"Then it's decided. Now, we'll have to be quick," Fedora was urging. "The guards will discover the theft very soon and the police will be swarming all over the place. We should just about have time to nip out, pick up a newspaper and get back. That should prove what I say is true."

She opened a drawer and pulled out a small brown piece of paper. "Here," she said, handing it to Jo who was nearest, "you will need this."

"What is it?" asked Jo, holding it out for Andy to see. It was a reddish-brown bank note unlike any they had seen before, but still vaguely familiar.

"Monopoly money," Andy suggested.

"Money, yes. What was known then as a 'ten bob note', worth ten shillings, half a pound. What would that be in 1986?" Fedora asked.

"50p"

"Fifty pence, ah yes, right!" she confirmed enthusiastically as she dusted down the front of her black trenchcoat and straightened the collar. "Now, you will both have to hold my hand," she announced.

For a streetwise kid like Andy, the idea of having to hold someone's hand rankled him to the core. Doubly so because he was a 10 year old boy. Triply so because Fedora was a girl. Sensing his reticence Fedora added: "If you don't have physical contact with me then you won't make the transition. Come on, I won't bite." She concluded with a friendly smile and a nod towards the exit.

Jo looked at Andy and shrugged.

Fedora adjusted her bracelet to a faint but distinct chirping sound, held out her hands and took a deep centering breath. Jo and Andy shared one more knowing look with each other. What lay ahead was uncertain, but they both knew that this might be their best chance of escape.

The three stood in a line facing the library wall, and the lights went out.

CHAPTER SEVEN:

THE NUMBER ONE

SUNDAY. 20TH MARCH 1966. 11.40am.

When their eyes adjusted the kids realised that they were indeed back in the darkened room again. Nothing had changed.

"How does she do that?" Jo whispered to Andy as they moved towards the doorway that led back to the corridor. The shrug that Andy gave in response was lost in the darkness.

Once in the corridor, back in the light, a feeling of familiarity and relief flooded through them. Though they hardly knew the building, compared to the futuristic antique library of Limbo, this place almost felt like home. In the distance they could hear the sounds of the church service still going on.

"What is that?" Andy asked his captor.

A faint chirp from Fedora's pearlescent gold bracelet drew her attention. She nodded almost imperceptibly.

"It's a Methodist service. This is Sunday after all," Fedora replied as though reading the information straight from a textbook. "And this is the home of the London Methodist Church."

"Oh yeah, of course, I forgot." Andy lied and shrugged to Jo behind Fedora's back. She nodded back, and surveyed their surroundings as they neared the head of the stairs.

"Ready?" she mouthed to him silently. He nodded again.

"NOW!" Andy roared, and both youngsters ran for all they were worth to the staircase and started down as fast as they could.

A couple of times they almost fell in their eagerness to escape, the sounds of their trainer soles squeaking on the floor, like squash players embroiled in a high paced rally, almost deafening as they reverberated off the stone walls. Jo braced herself as they crashed through the doors, half tumbling into the dazzling light and fresh air of the street outside.

They looked up, squinting at the bright sunlight. No trace remained of the downpour that had first ushered them into the hall. The pavement and the street were completely dry.

Opposite them a tea-stall had been set up and seemed to be doing good business, as a smartly dressed crowd formed an orderly queue.

"I had a quick look back when we got to the bottom of the stairs, I don't think she's following us," Andy informed his friend breathlessly. "Too fast for her. And you too," he added with a smirk.

"Get lost! You had a head start," Jo snapped back, before catching herself, "look, let's get out of here quick, just in case."

They ran to the corner and made their way hurriedly

back to the tube station. Frequent glances back revealed no pursuit, but in the haste and anxiety to make good their escape they took little notice of their surroundings, other than to note that it was far quieter than when they had made the same journey in the opposite direction earlier that morning.

As they reached the underground station Andy, out of habit, glanced at the newspaper stand for the comics. He had not seen any American comic books when he had given the racks a cursory look earlier, but now he noticed a whole line of them on a rack strung high above the vendor's head.

The boy stopped dead in his tracks, took a step nearer and looked up, wondering if they would have something of interest. The peril of his escape superseded by his all consuming passion. He had missed the Mart, and had money burning a hole in his pocket. To one side he immediately spotted a Spider-man comic; a reprint of Amazing Spiderman #1, its cover, a colourful picture of his hero trapped inside a glass jar with the Human Torch, blazing a fiery trail of red and yellow as he flew around him. The other three members of the Fantastic Four stood underneath.

"The Fantastic Four think I'm trapped," Andy mouthed, knowing the cover (and contents) by heart from his own reprint copy stashed away at home. "But they don't suspect my real power."

A large spot of colour announced "Two great Feature-Length Spiderman Thrillers!"

As was tradition with modern reprints like Andy's, words explaining such would be printed on the bottom- in this instance part obscured by the rack. Hoping to convert his companion to his comic cult, Andy pulled a handful of change out of his pocket. "How much is that one mate?" he asked politely. Usually they would cost him 40p, but as this one was a couple of years old (and a reprint), he hoped for cheaper.

"A Shillin'," said the newsagent dismissively in his thick East end accent. With a thin cigarette clamped between his chapped lips he seemed far more annoyed at the prospect of having to interact with a member of the general public than a man working a news stand outside a busy underground station should be.

"A wha'?" asked Andy.

The newsagent's face soured further.

"Bloody foreigners," he muttered under his smokey breath. "'Ere, lemme look." He gestured a nicotine stained finger towards Andy's handful of change. "There one 'a those," he said, contemptuously pointing to a five pence piece.

Andy sceptically handed over the silver coin, and the vendor casually tossed it into a metal tin below the counter with a satisfying metallic jingle. He lifted Andy's new purchase out of the stand with a small stick, and passed it to the boy.

"'Ere, your clothes are a bit funny," the grizzled old man said, finally looking the boy over, "but at least you've got a decent hair cut. Not like all those bloody 'ippies and weirdos we've been gettin' round 'ere lately."

Andy who'd spent most of his near 11 years ignoring the words of his elders had already switched his attention to the book. He licked his lips and fixed his eyes more closely on the object in his hands. His stomach lurched, and he felt a thrill run through him from the tips of his toes to his lightly trembling fingers. This comic book was not like his one at home. It didn't say "Marvel Tales" at the top. There was no date, no face of Spiderman in the top right corner. Andy felt a bead of sweat run down the small of his back as he read the bottom of the cover. Where it should have had the reprint logo instead it read:

'EXTRA ADDED ATTRACTION: SPIDERMAN MEETS THE FANTASTIC FOUR, AS "THE CHAMELEON STRIKES."'

The light shake of his hands became a more pronounced tremble.

"No way…" He whispered as he frantically (yet with absolute care), opened up the shiny cover. On the inside cover was an advert for encyclopaedias. Underneath that were the words:

"Copyright 1962 Vol.1 No 1 March 1963 issue".

What Andy held in his hands was no reprint.

American comics had always been difficult to acquire in England, often arriving in dribs and drabs, out of sequence, mostly months, and sometimes even years after their release Stateside. It was not inconceivable that this particular comic had arrived a few years late, TWENTY years late would be stretching it a bit.

These thoughts flashing through Andy's mind should've left him with a deep sense of foreboding, but equally, he was a ten year old boy holding a first edition of one of the most famous (and valuable) comic books on Earth.

"JO! JO! I've gorra a number one!" He wheeled around and danced with delight over to where Jo, her back to him, was stood, her attention engrossed by the large poster stuck to the wall. "Look! Jo! JO! A number one of Spidey! J..."

Her face was blank, her skin seemed somehow more pale as though the blood had been drained from it. He followed her glazed eyes to the poster.

"SPORT WITH STAMPS" Andy mouthed. "An exhibition of sporting stamps from around the world. Three million pounds of stamps on display. Unique collection. Central Hall, Westminster." His speech slowed as he reached the next line. "19th March 1966 - 26th March 1966." Andy's newly prized possession fell reflexively from his grip, flapping downwards to land splayed open on the concrete floor, his jaw dropped. Slowly he turned to look up at Jo. The facts were there written large in thick font and indian ink.

"It doesn't mean…" Andy began half heartedly.
Jo pointed to a coloured splash across the bottom of the poster.

SPECIAL ATTRACTION. On display the JULES RIMET TROPHY (The World Cup).

"We had better buy a paper," said Jo flatly. Spinning on her sneaker heel, she marched over to the newsagent, picked up a copy of the red topped 'paper 'The Daily Mirror', and thrust the ten-bob note into the calloused, print stained hands of the vendor.

"Oy! 'Aven't you got anyfin' less?" He snarled.
"No," Jo snarled back.

The man made a fuss of gathering together the change and with great deliberation counted out a pile of huge, unfamiliar, but distinctly English looking coins into Jo's hand. She held them out for Andy to see. The profile image of the

Queen was there, as expected, but she looked different, younger. The enormity of their situation was gathering like dark thunderous storm clouds. Andy looked at the header of the newspaper- the date: 20th March 1966, the black ink in stark contrast to the white paper. He looked closer at the pile of coins, and the young version of Queen Elizabeth embossed into them. He looked up at Jo.

"Time travel," she said.

Andy's eyes widened in a mix of understanding, terror and elation.

"I thought the Queen was looking a bit too cute," he said innocently.

The pair stood there in silence for a moment. Jo began to chuckle, a chuckle that quickly grew into a full blown laugh. Andy blinked twice, slightly taken aback for a moment, before getting swept up in the laugh himself.

"Bloody foreigners" The newsvendor mumbled, as he watched the young pair roll around in hysterics in the station entrance.

With composure restored, and Andy's prized find recovered from the floor, the pair sat on a step outside the station.

Andy idly flipped through the pages, and Jo surveyed her surroundings with fresh eyes. It was London, it was Westminster, with Big Ben towering overhead to prove it, but everything else was different. The clothes, the smells, the cars. Everything was less crowded, and yet somehow more formal. Jo had been raised on her parents stories of the swinging 60's, but here in the heart of central London, there were far more men in suits than women in flowery mini-skirts. And there were certainly no kids in tracksuit tops and trainers. Self conscious at how much they stood out, Jo smoothed the purple and black polyester of her top down, and folded her arms.

"We'll have to go back," Andy said resolutely, breaking the silence, and voicing what both were thinking.

"I know."

"If she goes without us we'll be trapped here forever."

"I know."

"We'll have no homes or families."

"I know."

"Or schools, or mates, or…"

Jo shifted to face Andy, and put a reassuring hand on his shoulder. "I know Andy. Besides, you know what's even worse?"

Andy's eyes darted side to side as he tried to contemplate any fate worse than those he'd already listed.

"Worse?"

"Yeah, much worse… I'll miss the match! My Dad'll murder me!" She said with a smile and a wink. The tension in Andy's body noticeably diffused.

"You'll miss the match, but at least you'll be able to watch England win the World Cup! That's only a few months away right?"

"I'd rather see Liverpool win a kickabout mate, and anyway, unless we convince Fedora to give it back there won't be a World Cup for England to win."

"Oh yeah, 'course!" Andy realised.

"Right," Jo said with authority as she stood up. "Let's go. Race you!" She said, bursting into a sprint.

"Ey!" Andy jumped up, and started his sprint, whilst also trying to take expert care in folding his comic away inside his jacket.

The pair raced back towards the Hall, and Jo quickly hit her stride, gracefully accelerating through the crowd. Without losing pace, she elegantly side stepped and hip swerved around the people in her path. By comparison to facing down defenders twice her size on the football pitch, this was a breeze. Andy, far more used to being chased than giving chase, struggled to make ground, raggedly dipping and dodging through foot traffic, bumping into important looking men and women, annoyed protestations lost in his wake. Once again the Hall and its ornate limestone doorway came into sight. Jo eased off her pace to allow Andy to catch up, "come on slow coach!" she teased. Andy, never one to shirk a challenge, increased his pace, and the pair once again clattered through the doors of the rear entrance. As they reached the bottom of the stairs, a white haired man in uniform appeared some way down the corridor.

"'Ere!" He shouted. "Whadder you kids want?"

"Keep going!" Jo said, grabbing a fistful of Andy's jacket and dragging him, lungs burning and feet pounding up the stairs two at a time. "If he catches us, we've had it!"

The pair bounded up the stairs, as loud footsteps and shouting raged behind them. They reached the landing, and with the screech of sneaker soles on stone floor, turned and headed to the second doorway. Their breath came hard, sweat beading along their hairlines, too scared to look back, the door swung open ahead of them.

Inside, Fedora stood waiting, her blonde hair dazzling against the dark interior, a slight wry smile momentarily touching the corners of her mouth. "Hurry," she urged.

The youngsters flew into the room and Fedora slammed the door shut behind them just as the security guard reached the top of the stairs, stomping his flat feet and breathing like an asthmatic hippo. He slammed a shoulder into the door with a painful wince, and it swung open wildly.

"Right…" he took a deep wheezing breath, "you… little… beggars…" But the kids were nowhere to be seen. He doubled over for a moment, putting his wrinkled hands onto his knees and fighting to get some much needed oxygen into his sweat coated, bright red face. The faint sounds of an unfamiliar hymn from the floor below finally began to replace the pounding of blood in his ears. Composure regained, he turned on a light switch next to the door to begin his search, "Mothering Sunday's, always the bloody same," he muttered, "bloody kids everywhere."

He opened the door to one of the exhibition rooms, turned on the light and immediately noticed dust covers strewn around the floor.

"Ooh you little blighters!" he exclaimed. "You'll have to put all these back before you leave 'ere, and don't think you won't be gettin' a clip round the ear too for yer troubles!"

He looked around the room, under, next to and behind the glass cases. Still no kids. Leaving the mess untouched, he made his way to the next room and opened the door. Inside it was absolutely pitch black.

"Come on you two," he said with a hint of trepidation in his voice this time. "You'll have me shot being in 'ere…" He turned on the lights and seeing the opened inner doorway, raced towards it, his heart rate spiking once again.

"Oh no, oh no, no, no!" He exclaimed. The lock had been forced, splintered wood lay on the floor, the door was ajar. Thoughts of disaster flooded his brain, a cold shot of adrenaline overriding the burning in his lungs, he raced over to the central exhibition case. It was still decked out in flags and rosettes of all the World Cup winners, though he noticed with a sinking feeling that one of them lay on the floor. He leapt to the back of the case. A small padlock had been snapped open. The World Cup was gone.

CHAPTER EIGHT:

FUTURE, PAST AND PRESENT

<u>Limbo. Outside the edges of known space and time.</u>

"Right, that's IT! What d'yer want with us?!" demanded Jo belligerently of their hostess as they re-emerged in the techno-library space she'd called Limbo.

"Oh nothing, I assure you, you're here quite by accident." Fedora said calmly, as she walked back over towards the central table.

"Then take us back!"

"She means forward," helped Andy.

"Shut up!" She barked at him. "Take us home!"

"She means London, not home."

"An-dy!" Jo said in absolute exasperation.

"Alright, only tryna help," he replied with an innocent shrug.

Fedora interrupted.

"I understand your desire to return to your own time but it's not quite that simple. Let me explain. Please sit down." She gestured encouragingly at the chairs around the dark, vintage looking mahogany table, with its eerily embedded lights.

    Jo blew an irritated sigh through her nose, walked to the table and stood there, arms crossed in an act of petulant defiance. Andy, despite being in his element, chose to side with his friend, mimicking her disgruntled stance alongside. Seeing them side by side, Fedora repressed a slight smile.

    "You will see from the books in this room," she continued, "that I am a student of the game. Futbol, Soccer, Association Football."

    "Togger, footy…" Andy suggested helpfully, and received an elbow to the ribs from Jo for his troubles.

    "Quite," Fedora confirmed.

    "Well," Andy said, a plan formulating in his little, devious mind. "If you come back with us to 1986, we'll take you the match with us won't we Jo?"

    "What match is that?" The older woman asked.

    "The one we talked about before," Jo piped up, "Liverpool are playing Southampton at White Hart Lane, look." From her back pocket she produced her match ticket, unfolded it and placed it down on the table. As her fingertips made contact with the glossy, thick paper stock, a constellation of lights on the table top ignited, and coalesced around the object. Jo and Andy reflexively closed their eyes to protect them from the brightness. When their eyes opened, a large, floating, semi-transparent recreation of the ticket hung in the air above the centre of the table. A pleasant if slightly stilted, disembodied voice began to dictate the typed text that adorned it's top side:

"LIVERPOOL V SOUTHAMPTON. FA CUP SEMI FINAL. WHITE HART LANE, SATURDAY, 5TH APRIL, 198.."

Jo withdrew her hand and the image blinked out of existence. Andy stared at her fingertips with wide eyes and gaping mouth.

"Whoa… magic fingers!"

Jo, desperate to continue her point, pushed down her equal feelings of amazement. "Err, yeah, White Hart Lane, that's why we're here in London y'see, to watch the match."

Andy noticed as the band of Fedora's wrist pulsed and chirped again, and watched as she nodded fractionally, as though confirming a point.

"Ah yes, White Hart Lane, home of Tottenham Hotspurs from 1899," she said without emotion before continuing, "The FA Cup Semi Final? Ooh yes, well if I can figure out what effect your arrival has had then maybe i'll take you up on that offer. You see, I really do love football, it's my life." Fedora's eyes were bright and shiny as she spoke. "In my time, however, it's not played very much at all."

"What? No football?" Despite this confirming what she'd read earlier, Jo still couldn't believe it. She'd had her own problems getting boys to let a girl join in their games, but the idea of not even having that, well that really struck a chord. "Not much of a future that then is it? How come?"

"Well. In 1966, the World Cup was stolen."

"Tell us news, not 'istory," Andy sneered. "WE'VE just stolen it!"

"Yes," Fedora continued. "You see I scoured every text, every video clip, every scrap of newspaper I could find, I studied football for years and fell in love with it. I longed to play the game and even set up a team. A few other groups have done the same, but it's just not catching on."

"The government have decided to ban all sports that we

can't do well in at the Olympics in order to improve our performance in the medals table. Football is seen as something of a 'wasteful pastime for the unwashed masses'. Those in charge see Olympic success as a way to improve our image around the world. Unfortunately grassroots football has had no funding for decades so there's no coaching, pitches or infrastructure left, and the idea of rebooting the professional game just doesn't have enough support either from sponsors or in Whitehall. Their plan is to finally ban it once and for all."

"But how are people meant to get good, or even fall in love with footy if they can't even play the thing?"

"Precisely. In my studies however, it became clear to me that the death of football in this country was directly attributable to the World Cup being stolen in 1966."

"But that's daft," Jo explained somewhat rudely, "the cup was found a week after it was stolen."

"What?" Fedora, for the first time, seemed genuinely taken aback.

"It was found by a dog or something. Honest. I read about it," Jo went on, and added patiently, "football's not dead."

"Let me think," said Fedora. "In my world, the trophy was stolen and never recovered. Look." She got up and searched through the shelves before pulling out a large hard backed book.

She returned to her seat and leafed through the volume. "Here, here we are." She placed it down on the table and a halo of white light formed around it. She gently touched the fingers of her slender right hand to it, and like before, in a swirl of light, the pages appeared in a ghostly, illuminated mirage above the table. As before, the disembodied voice began to speak in its calm, measured tone.

"Doctor Helmut Kaiser, Secretary of F.I.F.A. told the London Times on March 29th 1966 that he was 'especially sad for the English F.A. It is really a bad joke that in England such a trophy could be stolen and never found.' This hits at the heart of the matter. The national shame could not be overcome. England, the laughing stock of the world, failed to win a match in the ensuing tournament and the new cup made by British goldsmiths went to Argentina."

Jo went to interject, but Fedora cut her off with a raised hand.

"The following season, gates plummeted and televised football, with falling viewing figures, was scrapped. In 1970 an earthquake in Mexico led to the tournament being switched to Argentina. Three months before the tournament commenced Britain declared war on Argentina over the invasion of the Falkland Islands and did therefore not compete."

"Argentina defeated Brazil in the 1970 final and refused to compete in the 1974 competition if England were admitted. England were banned, the footballing world having little time for what had become a second rate footballing nation."

Jo and Andy sat there, enrapt in the story. Jo's head involuntarily shaking in disbelief. Fedora continued...

"Similarly the teams of the other home nations were ostracised. F.I.F.A. demanded that only one team be admitted to International events from the whole of the British Isles. Scotland, Northern Ireland and Wales all refused and were thrown out of both the International Federation (F.I.F.A.) and the European (U.E.F.A.)..."

Fedora removed her fingers from the page and slammed

the book shut. The voice cut abruptly short and the image hanging above the table broke up and disappeared with a faint static buzz. All that remained was a faint halo of light around the book on the table top.

"The RATS!" shouted Andy angrily, before adding, "What does 'ostracised' mean?"

"It's not true you dummy!" Jo said in exasperation. "The dog found the trophy, England won the World Cup in '66, Brazil won it in 1970, 'though me Dad says England were unlucky. There WAS an earthquake in Mexico, but only this year, 1986 and they are still having the tournament there and England are in it THIS SUMMER. AND Scotland. *AND Northern Ireland*," she added. "Kenny's gonna show the world how boss he is!"

"Kenny?" Fedora asked.

Fedora's bracelet chimed and shifted softly as she spoke, as though she were translating the noises into English.

"Ah yes, Kenneth Mathieson Dalglish, born March 4th 1951, began a senior career in football with Celtic in 1968, rising to his peak in 1972, scoring 29 goals in 53 appearances. His playing days however were cut short in 1976 when a serious knee injury sustained at the hands of Emlyn Hughes, whilst playing in an unsanctioned match between Scotland and England. Due to the game not having the backing of the U.E.F.A, the players were not insured to take part, and with no compensation to aid his recovery, the injury forced him to retire from action, aged 25 years old."

"WHAT!??? No way, not the King! If your world was robbed of Kenny, then it really is a nightmare!" Jo cried.

"Well it is different from yours. Football continued into this time, but without the TV deals and with less general interest there came an unstoppable rise in hooliganism; football terraces became a breeding ground for racist organisations like the National Front. Without international and European travel, Football became less a sport for the people, less about the competition, the escapism, the journey and instead became the home of local, small town mentality and violence. Football is no longer seen as England's greatest invention, it is seen as its greatest shame. With the global rise of American Football too, calls to shut the game down were seen by many as a blessed relief. Association Football may be dead, but the spirit of the game lives on, that's what I'm hoping to save. If I can revive England as a team, England, the founders of the game, I would be able to bring it back to prominence all over the world."

"So you decided to steal the World Cup? Isn't that what started all this mess? Aren't you going to be the cause of football's problems?"

"Well no. You see I had no way of knowing that an alternative world like yours existed, and besides, I figured that if the cup was stolen without a trace anyway, then it couldn't make it any worse if I got to it before the real thieves. They would probably only melt it down, whereas I plan to use it as a symbol to rally football supporters to the cause."

"But if you don't put it back you'll kill football in our time as well!!" Jo argued back.

"All I have to go on is your story, all I know for sure is that if I put it back, then my future will continue to come to pass." She cleared her throat. "It is clear that we come from parallel worlds that are seemingly identical until March 20th 1966. After that prime moment, the theft of the Jules Rimet trophy, they diverge. Now, either I'm in yours, or you are in mine. If we are in your world then we must put the cup back. If we are in mine then we must NOT put it back. But which one are we in? If we are in yours and I don't return the trophy, tyour future will be changed. If we are in mine and I do put it back then my future will be altered."

"Oh marvellous!" Jo sighed sarcastically. "Ab-so-lutely bloody marvellous!"

"Time travel and alternate universes! It's like the Flash!" Andy murmured, and then inspiration hit him. "Hang on, why don't you take us forward to 1986? If it's our world you can let us go and you can do what you like."

"Yeah," agreed Jo. "Why not? Well done Andy, I always knew you were a clever lad."

Andy winked, blew on his fingernails and pretended to polish them on the bobbled blue nylon shoulder of his jacket.

"Because," Fedora said, bursting their bubble, "whilst the cup is here in Limbo, the world I put you back in couldn't be yours. It might be mine, it might not, but it certainly couldn't be yours. No, the natural flow of time must be restored. The cup must be returned before you can be. That will also ensure that football survives, and flourishes, in one world at least. However, I must find a way to be sure that I am putting the cup back in your world and not mine."

"But if you put it back in your world, football will survive there as well," Jo countered.

"Perhaps. But I would also be returning to a world which wasn't mine, I may not even have been born. I'd be in Limbo for the rest of my life one way or another."

"Yeah well tough!" Andy said callously, "you started it!"

"Andy!" Jo admonished him, for the first time feeling some sympathy for Fedora, knowing that if the roles were reversed, she would do anything to protect the game she loved.

"There must be something you can do. Don't you get a manual or a handbook or somethin' with this time travel thing?" Jo asked.

Fedora laughed. "No. It's a time machine not a dishwasher. I didn't buy it."

"You robbed it?" Andy asked admiringly.

"No I most certainly did not," Fedora said with indignation in her voice. "Well, ahem, borrowed is a better way of saying it," She added with a playful smirk. "It's my father's you see. He's, well, one of those 'nutty professor' types. He invented it ages ago, but no-one could really see much use for it so it never caught on. It's been lying around for ages gathering dust. First of all I used it to make Limbo. Well, actually first of all I went back in time to watch the first World Cup Final, but second of all I used it to make Limbo, just to store my books really, out of the way. It's great for storage, you know, turns out there's infinite real estate in the void outside of time, and it stopped my mother complaining about the mess in my bedroom. Then, when I went to University and started studying football I realised that I could use it to help the game, to bring it back. It seemed so simple," she sighed. "Foolproof".

"Then we arrived," Jo stated.

"Yes," Fedora said sadly. "My Dad might be able to sort it out but, well I'm not sure I can get back to my own time now." She got up and paced up and down the floor for what seemed like an eternity.

Jo played with her plastic comb like it was a set of worry beads and watched. Andy's head remained on a swivel, still staring in wide eyed awe at every aspect of their surroundings.

Presently Fedora announced, "the best thing we can do is give ourselves time to think. It would be silly to rush into some action without being sure it's for the best. What do you say? I know I've gotten you into this mess but I'm sure I'll get you out of it in the end. Why don't we try being friends? We can relax, have some lunch..." She looked pleadingly at them.

Jo's anger had subsided. It was replaced in equal measure with fear, but also a growing empathy for the plight of their would-be captor. Andy, seemingly still lost in his science-fiction lover's fantasy, shrugged at Jo. She nodded back to him relentingly.

"Alright," Jo said, speaking for both of them.

"Oh good," Fedora said with a sigh of relief. "Now what would you like for lunch? Maybe afterwards we could do some time sight-seeing?"

Andy's eyes widened and his face lit up. "Time travel?"

"Yes Andy," Fedora replied with a pleasant smile. "Time travel."

"YESSSSS!!!!" He shouted in delight.

Even Jo struggled to repress a grin at her young partner's infectious enthusiasm.

CHAPTER NINE:

MIKE

<u>**Limbo. The timeless void between all moments.**</u>

"These nutty bits play havoc with me fillin's," announced Jo, waving a piece of fresh granary bread in the air.

"You should see what they make me eat at the remand centre. Quiche! Yuck! " Threw in Andy. "They say it stops you robbin'." He stuck his tongue out in mock disgust.

They were nearing the end of what had been a long, leisurely meal during which Fedora had shown great interest in her two companions' lives; where they came from, and what their interests were.

She was horrified to discover that Andy could not live with his parents, and blushed when he told her it was because of stealing. On the other hand she was thrilled not only to find that Jo was a keen football fan, but loved to play the game as well.

"I don't see why anyone should think your gender is important. Where I come from there are so few people playing, no-one cares whether you're a boy or a girl, just so long as you can kick a ball. In fact, I think I'm one of the better players,"

Fedora said boastfully.

"It doesn't sound too bad after all," said Jo as she swallowed another mouthful of bread. "Here, I mean, in my time, girls aren't allowed to play professional football with the boys. Has the Women's game survived in Europe? It's quite strong there now, I mean in the 1980's. I'm going to play in Italy one day," she said proudly.

"No, I'm afraid it's died all over."

"It's funny you know," Jo mused thoughtfully, "everyone keeps saying that hooliganism is going to kill the game. In your time hooliganism was just, well, an afterthought."

Fedora laughed.

"What's so funny?"

"Oh, I'm sorry. It's just that you make it sound as though you invented hooliganism."

"Thee did!" Andy butted in without looking up from the two small piles of coins, some old, some new, that he was perusing on the table between the dirty lunch plates.

"Liverpool supporters. I heard it on the radio. They started ripping up train seats in the sixties."

"No they didn't!" Jo growled. "It was Man United, me Dad said."

"Now, now, no arguing," Fedora interceded. "Actually, my research suggests that it started much earlier than that. I've got some data in the computer about it. I'll just go and check it, and prepare for our first trip. I'll only be a minute." And so saying she walked over to the doorway, waved her pearlescent golden bracelet over the lock, and left the library.

"What d'yer think?" Jo asked once she was certain they were alone.

"I think," Andy said, "that I may have given that fella a real shilling. I wondered why he didn't take any notice."

"What on earth are you chattin' about?" Jo said, wrinkling her freckled nose and raising an eyebrow.

"Look, some of these 5p coins are shillings. This one, look, it says on it, 'one shilling 1956'. I've never noticed before."

"Are you sure you've not got it mixed up with the funny money?"

"No, honest. I've been careful to keep 'em separate."

"Anyway," Jo shook her head, annoyed at being drawn into the sidetrack, "I don't mean that. What do you think about her; about this?" She gestured to the room.

"Oh!" Andy reacted thoughtfully. "I think she's okay yer know, and this sight-seeing thing sounds boss! We're going to travel. In time. Sound!"

"Well, I'm not so sure."

"You don't like her?" Andy was surprised.

"No, I do… It's just… Oh I don't know. I'm a bit scared. Where's it all going to end? WHEN is it all going to end?"

"Shall we go an' 'ave a look 'round?" Andy asked, with a look of playful mischief on his face. "She hasn't locked the door."

Jo mulled it over for a moment. "Okay."

Quietly, but directly, they walked over to the door, and indeed found it unlocked. Andy reached up on to his tip toes and opened it. Outside the door was a narrow, windowless, curved corridor. They followed it to the left and soon came to a blank wall. Turning around they retraced their steps and followed the wall as it curved back around the library in what appeared to be a semi-circle. Occasionally the wallpaper, thick gauge and sage green with golden and maroon leaf patterns threaded throughout (matching the side boards in the library), was broken by a door. Overhead a light with another intricate, stained glass lampshade shone a spotlight on the floor in front. There were three more doors further along.

    They opened the first one as quietly as they could. As it opened the light came on automatically and revealed a spacious kitchen with obvious signs of Fedora's lunch preparations. The next two doors revealed bedrooms. Plain walls, grey sheets, neat, tidy and as lifeless as a furniture catalogue, both looked as though they had never been used.

    As they reached the fourth door they saw Fedora through an open gap, bending over a small computer monitor, watching the square screen intently, the faint glow casting onto her delicate features. With a loud 'clacking' sound she punched more information into the machine using the thick, yellowing keyboard, and said "try that."

    Noticing her two new companions she beckoned them into the room, seemingly unconcerned about their wanderings. Andy, whose normal instinct when caught was to run for all he was worth, fought every fibre of his being this time. For kids whose technological exposure was limited to the living room TV set, and school calculators, they were fascinated by the boxy computer that sat on the desk. Jo had heard that schools in the posher districts of the city had a computer or two, but that was certainly not the case for hers, the device looked like something straight out of a science fiction movie.

    "I'm just trying to design some appropriate clothing for a couple of dates I quite fancy going to. It would not do for us to be too noticeable."

"Can we go into the future?" asked Andy excitedly, his flight urge now fully repressed.

"I'm afraid not Andy," Fedora replied, "until we are sure of whose future it is - yours, mine, or someone else's - we'll just stick to the past I think. We know for sure that your past and mine are identical prior to 1966 so we shouldn't do any harm watching a few football matches before that."

"Can we? Really?!" Jo's excitement bubbled over. Unlike Andy, those science fiction films held little interest for her, but being able to go and actually experience some of the greatest games in the flesh? THAT was something she could get excited about.

"Yes, it's what I'd always intended to do with the time machinery. I've really been looking forward to it. My chance to watch the greats- Matthews, Finney, Charlton…"

"Dixie Dean!" Andy piped up, pleased to have been able to drop an Everton legend into the conversation for a change.

"Exactly!" Fedora pointed to him with a grin. "The great players, the great matches! I've always wanted to go and see an FA Cup Final," she enthused.

"Yeah me too! Pity we can't go to the 1974 one, Liverpool versus Newcastle. Belter of a game!" Jo joined in.

"Don't worry, there are plenty of games to see in the past Jo. The Stanley Matthews Final in 1953 - Blackpool 4, Bolton 3. Or we could watch the first EVER final in 1872 between Wanderers and the Royal Engineers; or the first final at Wembley or…" Fedora's passion was infectious, Jo's eyes lit up as she imagined the sights and sounds, replaying the black and white footage she'd seen on the TV in her mind's eye. "… the first final in which teams wore numberson their shirts, 1933

- Everton wore 1 to 11, and Manchester City wore 12 to 22."

"I bet Everton won," said Andy who was less swept up in the football nostalgia and had been giving the computer a thorough examination, his nose practically squashed up against the screen.

"Yes. Everton 3. Manchester City nil." A deep, rich male voice answered from the machine. Andy jumped backwards in fright at the unexpectedness of it. It was the same voice as earlier in the library.

"The teams were…" the voice continued, seemingly unaware of the reaction it had caused.

"MIKE! That's enough," Fedora said curtly. "I thought I told you to keep quiet. I knew you would frighten them. Oh well, there's nothing else for it now. MIKE, this is Andy and Jo. Andy and Jo, please meet MIKE, he's my computer."

The youngsters stood open-mouthed. Andy, a child raised on incredible futuristic tales of talking robots and computers could barely contain himself. He'd had his suspicions that such a device might be within Fedora's employ. Jo, on the other hand, was taken aback, not just by the computer's existence, but far more by how much warmth and humanity there was in its tone. MIKE spoke again.
"I'm very pleased to meet you, Jo and Andy. If there is anything I can do for you, just ask."
"Th-thank you," Jo and Andy chorused.

"Hey! That gold thing on your wrist, when it bleeps, is that MIKE talking to you?" Andy asked, absolutely fizzing with excitement.

"Why yes," Fedora said, looking down at the golden bracelet on her left wrist. "How did you figure that out?" She seemed genuinely impressed.

"Oh, it's just like Luke and R2."
"Who?"
"Nevermind, what does MIKE stand for anyway?" Andy asked.
"Eh?" said Jo.
"Is it like, an, an.. anacron.."
"Oh," Jo interjected, finally understanding his question, "an acronym. He wants to know if the letters of his name mean anything."
"Yeah, like K.I.T.T, the car in Knight Rider; The Knight Industries Two Thousand." He said waving his hand in front of him as though reading the name from a plaque.
Jo rolled her eyes.
"Multi Interface Komputing Enterprise," he mused.
"Computing is spelt with a 'C' dingbat," Jo said sourly.
Andy pulled a tongue at her.
"No," MIKE responded, "it's just a name."
"Aww, that's a bit naff innit? What kind of super, talking computer doesn't have an anacro-thingy?"
"Hmm, interesting," MIKE posited thoughtfully.
"Massively intellectual Klothing Emitter" Andy said, "Oh, no, wait…".
Jo shook her head.
"Right," said Fedora brushing aside all these interruptions to return to her favourite topic. "Everton, Man City, was there anything else memorable about that game, MIKE?"
"Only that Dixie Dean and Matt Busby played on opposite sides," he replied, with the barest hint of a clipped, digital edge to his words that was most pronounced when joining the first and last names of the players.

"Urgh! Matt Busby and Dixie Dean!?" Jo said in horror, forgetting her fright and suspicion of the computer's voice.

"Well, Matt Busby did play for your beloved Liverpool F.C a few years later," Fedora informed the younger girl.

"Matt Busby? Nah!" Jo couldn't believe it. To her, Busby was forever associated with Liverpool's bitter rivals Manchester United. "Are you sure?"

"MIKE?"

"Yes, Miss Fedora is correct. In fact, he signed for Liverpool in 1936, and played 122 games before 1940 when the league was suspended because of the Second World War. He played several…"

"Okay MIKE, thanks. But what about Dixie Dean?"

"Bill Dean. Affectionately known as Dixie, started…"

"Not you MIKE. Jo, would you like to see Dean's famous sixtieth goal in one season?" she asked, and seeing the grimace on the girl's face, continued, "No? What about Hungary beating England at Wembley in 1953?" The young blonde woman seemed almost aglow with the possibilities.

"My Dad says the best match he's ever seen was Liverpool against Inter Milan in 1965, just after we'd won the cup," Jo offered, finally clocking on to the potential of their situation.

"Well, we could see that then!" Fedora beamed.

"Honest?"

"Sure, why not?"

A huge smile spread across Jo's face.

"I'm sure MIKE has the coordinates, and then maybe on to a game of my choosing," Fedora said, beginning to map out a plan of action. "Andy, you're quiet. Is there anything, anywhere you would like to go and see? MIKE can place us just about anywhere if he has a date and time."

"Erm. How about a few shops?" Andy asked.

"Shops?"

"Yeah, you've made me miss the Comic Mart, the least you could do is buy us a few comics!"

"Andy! Don't be so cheeky!" Jo interjected. "You've got your own money. Anyway, you've got that 'Fantastic Spiderman thingy' one already haven't you?

"AMAZING Spider-man," he corrected, "and yeah but I could find some others, there's loads of famous ones out there Amazing Fantasy, Action Comics, even Amazing Spider-man number 2 would be a dream now i've got the first one. Oh, but I haven't got any more of that funny money left have I?" Andy said sadly, "Apart from a few shillin's."

"That's alright," Fedora announced. "I suppose I do owe you both a present or two but what's this about comics Andy?"

"Oh it's just his stupid daft books, take no notice," Jo said dismissively.

"They're not stupid!" Andy said, puffing out his chest, and opening his jacket. "I'll get a fortune for this when I get home," Andy said, indicating the colourful magazine he still had carefully placed inside the lining.

"I thought you said you would never sell it," Jo reminded him.

"Yeah, well," Andy said, rolling his shoulders, and re-zipping up his jacket, "I won't, but it's still worth loads of dough."

"Just stop a moment," Fedora implored, raising her

voice. "You've lost me."

Andy explained about his passion for American Comics and about his collection of them.

"Panelology," the computer's voice announced.

"Panelology?" Three voices chorused in return.

"Panelology. The study of comic books and comic strips." The rich voice replied. Again to Jo it sounded so real, so human but its slightly staccato rhythm almost betrayed its electronic origin.

"Go 'ead!" said Andy with a satisfied nod.

"I'm impressed," said Jo. "Andy's a pan-el-ol-o-gist then? Not just a collector of funny books," she said struggling over the collection of syllables. Andy seemed pleased with his new official title.

"If we get the chance then okay," Fedora told the boy. "Anyway, let's get going. For 1965 I think you'll get by with the jeans you're wearing. A duffle coat each should do the trick."

MIKE's screen lit up in full colour and two wireframe drawings of hooded coats, one bigger than the other, and several sets of figures appeared.

"Duffle coats?" The youngsters couldn't believe the suggestion. "I'm not wearing one of them!"

"But you must. They'll cover your modern clothing and keep you warm."

"Warm!" Andy burst out laughing.

"What's so funny?"

Andy was too busy giggling to answer, so Jo, who had slightly better control answered. "Well, there was a full house at that Inter Milan game, I'm sure of it."

"Yes?"

"You've never been in a big crowd have you? The crush, the sweating bodies…" she chuckled, "we'll die of heat!"

"Fascinating." Fedora considered. "Alright, what do you suggest, but remember, we're talking about 1965, and the sanctity of the timeline. Being inconspicuous is paramount."

"A couple of red football shirts and if you could put a Liverpool badge on them all the better."

On the screen, text based fact files with three dimensional images of Liverpool kits, stretching all the way back to the club's creation in 1892 flicked past, almost too quick to process. After a moment, it settled on 1965 and a kit of all red socks and shorts, and a red shirt with a white circular collar and a white oval badge on the left breast. The badge had a Red Liverbird at its centre and the letters 'L.F.C' in red stitching.

"Can I have a red and white scarf as well?" Jo asked.

"Certainly."

"I thought you didn't wear colours," Andy said slyly.

"I do at home. Anyway, I'm not likely to be beaten up by Italian Boot Boys am I, you daft dope!"

Andy pulled a face. "Well, I don't want one. Have you got any in blue?"

"Andy!"

"Only joking. What colour do Inter play in anyway?" He poked, knowing the answer full well.

Jo sighed, "Blue, but it's blue AND black stripes, and anyway, you can wear colours at Anfield, but you DEFO can't wear away colours, ESPECIALLY not blue!" She poked back.

"Come on," Fedora cut across the bickering. "The outfits will be ready by now."

"Ey? How do you do that?" asked Jo.

"Oh it's MIKE really. He works out designs based on photos, magazines, old videos, even descriptions in books and newspapers, and then programmes our fabrication machine to run them off. The results should be pretty authentic."

"Wow!" Jo whistled, "that sounds like it would come in dead 'andy!"

"Dead Andy?" MIKE's voice boomed out around them in the corridor as they made their way towards the clothing room. "I have scanned his vitals and can assure you that Andy is in fact alive and well…" Jo and Andy both laughed.

"No, it's just an expression, oh never mind."

"Curious," the computer replied.

"That's okay MIKE," his owner helped out. "We'll do some more work on your colloquial English when we've sorted this mess out. Anyway, here we are."

She led them into another room not unlike the last. This one however was bare except for a metal bench laid out across the wall opposite the door. The other two walls on either side were lined with a series of thin doors, each of which was covered by a full-length mirror and ringed by recessed lights.

The wall in front of them, behind the bench, had an array of slits, of varying sizes, that looked like letter boxes. At either end of the bench were metallic hatches, with vertically sliding doors, similar to dumb waiters. Beneath each a thin conveyer belt ran across the length of the bench.

"Manufacturing complete." MIKE confirmed.
The left hand door opened automatically and out slid three long sleeved red football shirts, exactly like the ones they'd seen on screen earlier, and a single red and white knitted scarf. They came to rest in the centre of the bench.

Jo ran over, with an excited spring in her step, and picked up the middle shirt, running the thick cotton between her fingers, and examining the stitch work of the crest with awe. She grabbed the scarf and tied it around her right wrist.

"Is that how they are worn?" Questioned Fedora, clearly surprised.

"Nah!" said Andy scathingly. "No-one does that anymore."

"They used to do it a few years ago," Jo explained politely, giving the lad a withering glance. "I never did, but I always wanted to."

"No-one's gonna wear them like that in 1965 are they?" Andy taunted.

"That's alright. Maybe I'll start a trend" she replied, sticking out her tongue and smiling.

"Excellent. Well then," Fedora gestured with a wide smile. "Shall we?"

CHAPTER TEN:

HERRERA'S ROBOTS

<u>Tuesday. 4th May 1965. 5:30pm. Anfield.</u>

At first everything seemed so familiar. There was the old school with the minaret shaped bell tower, the pub on the corner nicknamed "the Flat Iron" because of its shape, and the same row of terraced houses stretching away down Anfield Road towards the football ground.

Despite warming to Fedora, Jo had still been tense and worried by this whole adventure. Its very unusualness disturbed her. Now for the first time she relaxed.

A wave of excitement rushed through her as she became aware of the crowds of people, mostly adorned in red and white, making their way noisily in the direction of the stadium a quarter of a mile away.

And that was the first jarring note. Like putting on a coat identical to your own but knowing instantly that it belongs to someone else. This felt wrong.

"What time is it?" She grabbed Fedora's elbow to get her full attention.

"Now you mean? Hmm, well it's 5:31 in the afternoon. Why? I'm sure we're in plenty of time."

"It's just the crowds," she said with awe in her voice. "Me Dad always said they locked the gates hours before the game." She didn't add that she had never really believed him. Getting into the ground early was something Jo liked to do, seeing the players in the warm ups, feeling the growing atmosphere, but that usually meant 45 minutes before kickoff, and even then there was practically no-one else around. For there to be THIS many people, a full TWO HOURS before the game started, was startling. But this only served to whet her appetite for the match ahead.

"Can I have some chips?" Andy asked, almost vibrating with excitement as his attention was pulled in a million different directions, "there's a chippy just 'round the corner. I can smell that it's still there."

"You've just had lunch," said Fedora in amused disbelief, but rummaged in the large, leather, rectangular shaped hand bag she had slung across her left shoulder, and handed the lad some money.

"Is any of this familiar?" She asked of the two future locals as she looked around.

"Yeah," said Jo, "nearly all of it. There are a few things different but I can't quite put my finger on them. I'm sure that wasn't there though," and she pointed to a large sign of white lettering on black that covered the wall next to the pub. 'James Whittaker and Sons. Funeral Directors' it said clearly.

"Is there anywhere that I can purchase a newspaper?" Fedora asked.

"There was a shop - well, there will be - just along there past the old Police Station." Jo pointed along Anfield Road.

"Okay. You go for your chips and I'll meet you outside

the police station," Fedora suggested. "Don't be long."

Inside the shop, the air was thick with the smell of batter, and the din of excitable football chatter.

"Eh look," said a voice above the din in the small, packed fish and chip shop. "It's Saint John!"

All heads turned towards the young, red-shirted duo in the doorway. The room filled with laughter as they noticed the vague resemblance between the small, crew-cutted Andy, and Liverpool's idolised Scottish centre forward, Ian St. John.

"I knew I should've worn blue," Andy hissed between clenched teeth as they took their place in the queue. "Saint John, eurgh, he's a divvy."

"Shut up you," Jo hissed back and gave him an elbow to the ribs.

"Ey Saint, what's the score gonna be?" another comedian in the crowd asked.

"Six-nil."

A huge cheer went up.

"To Inter," Andy added with a sneer.

"Andy!" Jo screamed at him in horror, immediately noticing how loud she sounded in the silence that had fallen. She laughed to cover her embarrassment, and clipped her young friend around the ear.

"Take no notice, he's only joking- regular little comedian he is."

There was a roar as fresh chips were thrown into the hot fat followed by a loud sizzling noise.

"Well he looks more like St. John than Jimmy Tarbuck," the voice announced and laughter filled the shop again. Andy dug his hands into his pockets with a huff. An old lady in a grease covered brown tabard and flowered head scarf handed him a newspaper-wrapped bundle of chips over the counter.

"There you go Saint," she said with a wink and a smile. The crowd riled up again, and this time even Andy cracked a smile.

As they were leaving the shop with their food, Jo swallowed hard, took a deep breath, turned to the crowd and announced "Liverpool will win three one, and Hunt, Callaghan and St. John will score. Bet yer!"

Again the whole shop, staff included, sprang into cheer and started chanting, "Liv-er-pool! Liv-er-pool! Liv-er-pool!"

Andy stuck his head back in through the door, "And you'll lose the second leg three-ni..." A hand appeared above his head, grabbed his earlobe and dragged him away before he could finish.

They met up with Fedora outside the police station that was not as old as Jo had suggested and was clearly still used by the police.

"It's still open," she indicated her surprise, and a passing constable said, "Of course it is love, police stations are always open, twenty four hours a day."

"That's what you think," Andy said quietly.

As the policeman walked away Jo explained for Fedora's benefit that in their time, the building they now stood in front of was indeed closed.

"Well it's not a police station anymore, they use it for something else; I'm not sure what though."

They walked up Anfield Road with the ever thickening crowds. Jo could hardly believe she was twenty one years in the past, eight whole years before she was even born. At first glance everything looked the same but with a deeper inspection, the changes become more evident. There was an old fashioned uniformity about all the houses; old style doors, old windows and curtains instead of the varied modern flourishes that existed in the future. Above the red brick houses stood long lines of H-shaped television aerials atop the dark slate roofs.

As they reached the top of Utting Avenue the changes came thick and fast. They had already passed a well preserved St. Simon and St. Jude Church whose blackness stood out in the predominance of red brick. Now they saw Utting Avenue itself, lined with cars the likes of which the youngsters had never seen. Jo and Andy recognised the badges of Ford and Vauxhall, but the shapes and even the colours of pale blue, light creme and green seemed totally at odds with what they were used to. Dark green buses with openings at the rear and drivers stuck in cabins at the front, poured hordes of football fans onto the pavement, and then turned to return for another load down the other side of the dual carriageway.

Ahead of them, above the milling crowd and the terraced streets that fell away to the left, a huge concrete pillar rose into the sky. An array of lights set in a square could be seen perched at the top.

"Gosh!" said Jo. "You know I never thought about us having flood lights." And she explained to Fedora that in the future, the lights that Anfield will have are along the tops of the two stands.

The many changes to the ground became a major topic of conversation as the minutes passed while they awaited the kick-off. Fedora's newspaper, 'The Liverpool Echo and Evening News' had informed them that they would gain admission to the Paddock or ground by paying at the turnstile. The trio queued up briefly, slid their money across the small worn, wooden counter to the operator and pushed through the cold metal turnstile with a satisyingly heavy "kerchung" sound as it rotated around. Once inside they took up a position on the famous Spion Kop, where Jo said they would get the best view. Nevertheless, Andy, the shortest of the three by a foot, had to sit on one of the rounded, metal crash barriers that were dotted throughout the stand, in order to get a decent sight of the pitch, while his companions stood in front on tip-toes.

As Jo explained some more of the differences in the modern Anfield, and Andy struggled to hold and read the broad pages of the non-tabloid newspaper, the crowd filled up around them. Various chants and songs rang around the ground, none of them familiar to children of the eighties, and a tension filled the blue-grey tinged swirl of cigarette smoke coalescing above their heads.

"At least the Kemlyn Road Stand is the same," said Jo, pointing to the cantilever on their right. "Look, they must be Italians," she said, pointing over to a large group of supporters, waving elaborately embroidered flags and banners, who sat at the near end of the particular stand she was talking about.

"Listen to this," said Andy, awkwardly folding the newspaper into some sort of order, and reading out loud.

> "All Europe has eyes on Anfield tonight to see
> If Liverpool F.C can become the second team
> to beat European Cup holders Inter Milan who
> sustained their first defeat in the tournament
> at Ibrox Park Glasgow in the quarter finals. It
> didn't matter much as 'Herrera's Robots" ...

Andy laughed out loud at the name before continuing.

> "As 'Herrera's Robots' had built up a 3-1 lead at their San Siro stadium in the first leg, but at least this result in Scotland showed that Inter were no longer invincible."

"Lets 'ave a look," asked Jo, taking the oversized 'paper from Andy.

> "Many soccer men abroad will be rooting for the F.A Cup Winners too, because semi-final victory for Inter would mean that the holders play the final on their own ground - a ruling which is regarded as grossly unfair."

"The rats!" she swore. "The Italians are still getting away with that! We had to play Roma on their own ground in the final in 1984 as well." And then as an afterthought and oblivious to the strange looks the man next to her was giving, she added, "we beat them anyway."

"My Dad used to play for Roma," Andy announced.

"What?" Fedora was more than surprised.

"Don't be daft," said Jo and gave him a push that meant she quickly had to grab his shirt front to stop him from falling backwards off his perch.

"Ey! He did too!" Andy insisted with a mischievous smile, "Royal Oak Muirhead Avenue - dead good they were."

At this point the crowd began to chant "Mussolini's dead, Mussolini's dead, ee-ay-addio, Mussolini's dead."

The Italians in the crowd rose to their feet and applauded. "What position did *he* play?" Andy asked, still very much in a joking mood. The crowd within ear shot started to laugh.

The pearlescent bangle on Fedora's wrist chimed, and she nodded. "Thanks MIKE. He was the Italian leader…"

"I know, I know," said Andy. "He was a dictator in the war. It was supposed to be a joke."

"Oh!" Fedora said and frowned at her wrist.

As the tension and excitement reached fever pitch, the noise and cigarette fumes rose, and the crowd began to sway forward and back on the terraces, the Italian team burst onto the pitch through a crowd of photographers, policemen and officials. The night air was instantly filled with loud 'boo'ing' and jeers, but the Inter Milan team, dressed in white shirts with a diagonal blue and black flash from left shoulder to waist and black shorts, commenced an orderly kickabout at the Anfield Road end, the opposite end of the ground to where the time travellers were perched. The pristine white of their shirts and the verdant grass seemed to glow under the powerful floodlights as the sun began to set in the background.

The home crowd broke into a chorus of "Go Back to Italy", sung to the tune of 'Santa Lucia'.

The minutes passed, the temperature rose and the Kop swayed in anticipation. The huge crowd seemed to hold its breath as the noise died to a relative whisper; an expectant buzz of anticipation ran through the spectators.
Suddenly a HUGE, deafening sound erupted. The crowd went wild with delight. The whole of the Spion Kop, craning on tip toes to get a better view, seemed to lurch forward and people went hurtling headlong down the steps. As the sway reached its zenith, the people, no longer compelled forward, raced back totheir places.

Andy, still perched atop his barrier, smiled as Jo and Fedora returned to him. "Welcome back!" he said playfully.

Jo smirked at him. She had never been in a crowd so large and a trace of fear edged in with her excitement, until she looked at Fedora, who seemed to be in complete shock. Fedora was wide-eyed and rosy cheeked, swept away both figuratively and literally by the visceral nature of her surroundings.

"Not like that in your books is it?" Jo prodded.

Fedora blew a loose strand of blonde hair from her eyes, and tucked it behind her ear as a broad smile spread across her face.

"Not quite," she said with a chuckle. Andy, perched like a King above the turmoil, seemed delighted.

Just as it seemed impossible for any more noise to be generated, the roar increased.

"What is it? What is it?" Fedora questioned with a mix of alarm and excitement, adrenaline coursing through her body.

"It's the F.A Cup!" Jo answered. "Shankly, the manager, got Gordon Milne and Gerry Byre who were injured to carry the cup around the ground. Remember, they only won it three days ago!" Jo found herself almost screaming to be heard. "It's driving the crowd mad, the Italians are scared to death!"

As she spoke, Andy and Fedora could see two men in dark suits carrying a gleaming silver cup around the perimeter of the pitch.

"That must be Gerry Byrne nearest the pitch, with his arm in a sling," Jo informed them further. "He broke his collarbone in the third minute of the Cup Final but still stayed on! He even laid on the first goal in extra time!"

"He must be cracked," shouted Andy. "Why didn't he just go off??"

"Well, they never had substitutes back then, err…

now," she said, catching her error in tense with a roll of the eyes. "If he'd gone off, we'd've had to play the game with ten men."

The trio waited as the trophy got nearer and nearer, with the Kop getting wilder and wilder; a rising tide of twirling scarves, and voices and humidity, until it was immediately below them.

"Now THAT'S a symbol of football for ya," Jo told Fedora, leaning in closer so she could be heard over the din. Fedora's eyes gleamed. The Cup made its way full circle, the Anfield crowd at fever pitch before a ball had even been kicked.

The decibels dropped as the teams lined up, only to return with a vengeance as the shrill sound of the referee's whistle pierced the air, and the game got under way.

Despite knowing the result, Jo was as excited and tense as anyone in the ground. She looked around at the players in their all red kits and saw in the flesh men she held in awe, but knew only in legend. Ian St. John, Roger Hunt, Peter Thompson, Ian Callaghan and Ron Yeats, the colossus at the heart of the defence. Even Tommy Smith, who she had seen on video scoring in her favourite European Cup Final in 1977 had retired by the time she had persuaded her father to take her to her first match. Now here he was, probably the youngest player on the pitch.

As these thoughts raced through her mind, Liverpool's left back, Ronnie Moran standing in for Byrne, slipped and Tommy Lawrence, the stocky goalkeeper in his green shirt, had to race from his goal to stop the onrushing Inter centre forward. Moran, who Jo knew as one of Liverpool's coaches in her time, actually didn't look that much younger. It occured to Jo that, although she knew the broad strokes of the game, the fine details were about to unfold before her.

Geoff Strong, a player Jo was largely unfamiliar with, pushed the ball to Callaghan on the right wing. Attacking the goal away from the Kop, the tireless scouse winger approached the Inter full back, and as another defender moved across to cover, he crossed the ball hard and low towards the penalty spot. Roger Hunt, quickest to react, crashed the ball right footed across himself into the left corner past the helpless Italian goalkeeper in black. Ecstatic, the forward immediately wheeled away out of the box, twice jumping and punching high into the air in celebration before his teammates engulfed him. The Kop bounced with joy, a sea of bodies and flashes of red and white. The crowd reached new heights of passion, and Jo, who had never realised that the goal came so early, was as surprised as anyone, and she screamed in authentic joy with everyone else around her, in the melee of bodies.

Still tottering on her toes, craning her neck to see, and holding onto the barrier behind her to stop from being tossed around in the seemingly endless sways, she fixed her attention back on the pitch.

Yeats strode like a giant to stop a move developing on the right and Jo shouted, "TACKLE 'IM!" in unison with some 30,000 others around her, all the while knowing that the tackle would be missed, the ball would be cut back to an unmarked Mazzola at the back post for Inter to equalise.
A collective groan of annoyance in the crowd was quickly replaced by the resolute rumblings of defiance. It had been a breathless first ten minutes of the game, even Andy atop his perch was so absorbed that he forgot to make his usual jibes.

The Italians began to dominate the game with their

playmaker spreading passes to his forwards from deep positions. Twice the outside right had good chances but missed them, and then Liverpool were awarded a free kick ten yards outside the penalty area.

Jo's father had used this goal as a bedtime story so often throughout her childhood that she knew exactly what was coming and was bursting to tell someone. "Watch Callaghan," she shouted to Fedora, "the number seven." She mouthed the words deliberately to make them more intelligible in the clamour.

A three man wall of white, black and blue lined up, with one man facing the goalkeeper, getting positional instructions. In line with the wall, five or six yards nearer the centre of the goal, Roger Hunt took up position, his back to goal.

Callaghan ran to take the kick, but skipped over the ball and ran past the outside of the wall - a feeling of intense glee stood the hairs on Jo's neck on edge. Smith pushed the ball to Hunt who clipped it behind the wall and into the path of Callaghan, who hammered it under the diving goalie.

Jo danced in undisguised delight, and Fedora whose eyes were seemingly even wider still than before, turned to look at her in amazement as they were swept along the terrace, like excitable buoys on a writhing ocean of joy.

Liverpool now gained the upper hand. Smith had a shot pushed over the bar and then Lawler, the right back who was playing brilliantly, ran half the length of the field and scored.

Fedora again jumped up in wild celebration with the crowd, but Jo stood there with a puzzled look on her face.

"What's wrong?" Fedora asked, shocked at her young companion's reserved reaction.

"That never happened," came her confused reply.

"What? Oh, look, it's been given offside."

"Oh thank goodness," Jo said with relief, getting another funny look from the man next to her.

Jo relaxed again. "Ey Ref! That was never offside!!!" She bayed at the referee, and Fedora smiled.

The game continued to be one way traffic in the second half despite another early slip by Moran. When Hunt ran on to a Smith pass, pulled the ball inside a defender and shot powerfully with his left foot, Jo watched as St. John tucked away the rebound off the goalkeeper, right under the noses of the rapturous Kop. Once again Jo and Fedora found themselves compelled forward down the stand towards the action, the Kop like a living, breathing behemoth taking deep inhales and exhales along with the action. With the win all but secured, once again "Go Back To Italy" was chorused around the old ground, reverberating off the wooden rafters and steel girders in the Kop roof. Liverpool in control, passed the ball around, sapping the last of the fight from their opponents. Those pristine white shirts, darkened by mud, grass and sweat as the final whistle blew to the jubilation of those in attendance.

At the end of the game, a torrent of singing and shouting people poured down the steep steps out of the ground, and Fedora became concerned that they would lose each other.

As she voiced her fears to the youngsters, Jo suggested that they once again meet by the police station.

"I've a better idea," Fedora told them. "Hold tight." Bodies crowded all around them. Pressure from all sides pushed them together. Suddenly a small gap appeared and was just as quickly swallowed up.

The disappearance of three people made little

difference and they were not missed amongst the celebrations. A happy refrain and the repeated words, "Here we go, here we go, here we go!" hung in the air, as the gathered throngs of revellers contemplated with misplaced optimism the prospects of a European Cup Final appearance that was not to be.

JOHN. J MACHIN

CHAPTER ELEVEN:

HOOLIGANISM

Saturday. 19th March 1892.

It was dark. Very, very dark. For Andy, that was the surprise. All his short life he had lived in a city that was well lit at all times. Even in the dead of night, the street lights were always bright and the stars above were mere pinpricks in a man-made electric fog.

But here!

The time travelling trio had swung through the time effect into a blackness deeper than the room in Central Hall, deeper than anything Andy had ever known or thought possible. There was soft, damp grass under their feet, and they appeared to be in the middle of a small park, with no houses nearby shedding any light for them. And then Andy looked up.

His mouth fell and an audible gasp dropped from his open lips. The sky was a vast dome above him, and the dome was filled, crowded, bursting with points of light, some bright, some almost dazzling.

He remembered the fireworks display he had seen in Sefton Park the year before, and how bright light had splashed itself across the sky, thus revealing an enormous amphitheatre of onlookers for a split second before the darkness reclaimed them. But this! It was like a still photograph of an even greater fireworks display, and it thrilled him with a realisation of something he knew had always been there, hidden from his view, but now was revealed in a glory far beyond his imaginings.

The modern lad gazed upwards, dazed, and felt an overwhelming urge to lie down on his back and look upwards forever.

"Wonderful isn't it?" Fedora's silky voice slipped elegantly into the silence beneath the dazzling display above them. "There's only gas powered lighting, which just can't compete with that. Absolutely marvellous."

A crashing sound starkly interrupted their contemplation, and broke Andy's star-gazing reverie.

"What's that?" He asked, shaking his head and returning his attention back to earth, "Shhh, listen."

Another crash of breaking glass reached them and a cacophony of shouts and cries could be heard behind it. Now Andy was surprised that he'd not heard it sooner.

"What is it?" he repeated with a hushed tone.

"That, I think, is what we're here for," Fedora declared. "Good old MIKE, spot on." Her bracelet gave off a positive sounding chirp in response.

"Yeah, sound, great, but what is it?" Andy asked for a third time.

"Football hooliganism circa 1892!" Fedora announced proudly.

"Yer wha'?" Chimed in Jo, who had been quietly surveying her surroundings until now.

Fedora's bracelet chimed again.

"1892. The earliest incidence of football hooliganism I've yet managed to track down. MIKE uncovered one in December 1906 when the officials needed police protection and were stoned by a large mob after Crewe Alexander beat Paulton in the F.A Cup. Apparently the crowd followed the team to their hotel and attacked them. One player was knocked unconscious by a stone." Fedora said with far too much enthusiasm for such a moody tale. She saw the bemused looks of her fellow travellers, realised her over exuberant mistake, coughed and continued.

"Well yes, anyway, if we'd chosen to see that we could have followed the team to the railway station where the lights had been turned off so that they wouldn't be seen by the murderous mob." Fedora mouthed the last words slowly for dramatic effect.

"Oh. Yeah." Jo said, not convinced that this was a good idea.

"Anyway," Fedora continued, "I thought we'd see the earliest one I could find, though to be honest I suspect there has been hooliganism since the first day a ball was kicked. Victorian society as a whole certainly had a large problem with hooliganism and street rioting. It seems to me though that football hooligans originally attacked players. Later on they switched to attacking each other. You can decide for yourself which is best. They are both pretty unpalatable."

"Does that mean you don't like them?" Andy asked.

"Of course I don't like them. Mindless violence by mindless people. I just thought you should be aware that the problem has been around for a very long time without a solution."

"So this is an attack on a player?" Jo asked. "But it's night time, no-one can be playing now."

"Sort of," Fedora explained. "In the 1890's the Birmingham clubs were very strong."

"Birmingham?" Jo sighed. "Is that where we are?"

"Yes indeed. In 1892 Aston Villa and West Bromwich Albion both reached the F.A Cup Final. They were deadly local rivals and Villa lost three-nil. Villa were the top team in the country at the time so their fans couldn't believe it. They reasoned therefore that the only way their great side could have lost was if their goalkeeper, who had played badly, had taken a bribe to throw the game."

Fedora ushered them out of the small recreation ground and towards the din in the distance.

They walked down a narrow, cobbled street, keeping themselves tucked close to a brick wall which ran the whole length of the road.

Soon, in the glow of two pools of yellow light, they could make out a large crowd. They could hear chanting and swearing and the sound of breaking glass as bricks were torn from the ground and hurled at the windows of the large public house they were milling around outside of. One particularly enraged (and acrobatic) fan was swinging on the pub sign suspended over the main door.

"These people," Fedora whispered, "are from the Wellington Road end of the Villa ground."

Andy, whose eyes lit up at the carnage unfolding before him, was reminded of a natural history programme he'd seen on television, one where some man in khaki shorts had gone in amongst the gorillas and whispered his commentary on their mating habits.

"And that," Fedora was saying in hushed tones, "is the pub run by Jimmy Warner, the Aston Villa 'keeper. By the end of the night he won't have a window left."

"Or a customer," Jo added.

Fedora laughed softly. "Yes, or a customer."

"They attacked his pub though? How horrible is that?" Jo was disgusted.

"Okay. Hold tight," Fedora ordered, and made several deliberate taps and strokes on the faintly glowing bracelet. "Thanks MIKE."

With a faint whooshing sound, the cool night around them vanished, and Limbo flashed back into existence.

"Right then, my choice. Follow me!" Fedora said cheerily.

Fedora led her young companions back to the fabrication room. There on the bench were three heavy overcoats, three pairs of leather boots and three flat caps.

Once dressed, Jo checked herself out in the full length mirrors. Alongside her, Fedora had slid out a wheeled tray from one of the mirrored doors, and was reapplying costume makeup, and a moustache similar to the one she'd had when they first met.

"Right," Fedora announced, "Now we're suitably dressed for the nineteenth century, we can go to my match choice without raising a fuss."

Andy stood in the middle of the room behind Jo. He shrugged his shoulders inside his large woollen overcoat, and placed both hands disconsolately on his peaked cap.

"I look like me Granddad," he sighed. "Do I have to wear these boots?" He asked stomping them loudly on the wooden floor for effect.

"Yes you do. And think yourself lucky. Some of the children we'll see won't have any shoes at all. They'd give anything for those."

"They can have them," Andy harrumphed.

"Well don't go giving them away. The real things would be made of leather and hob-nails and weigh a ton. If we leave synthetic fabrications behind… Well, who knows what harm it would do," Fedora warned.

"Why are you dressed as a man again?" Jo asked.

"Well, in Victorian times women just didn't go out on their own, especially at night."

"Sounds just like 1986 to me," Jo suggested sourly.

"Or 1996, or 2006 for that matter," Fedora informed her with a knowing shake of the head, "only in the 1890's it really would've been considered unusual as well as dangerous, so I thought it best if I be a man again. It's surprising, and if i'm wholly honest, rather annoying what you're able to do more easily if you're a man."

"Yeah, like play footy," Jo agreed.

"Yes and most pertinently, take two children to a football match in 1895."

"I wish I was a man," Andy announced, puffing his chest up to try and fill the oversized coat. The two women laughed and shared a knowing look.

"Okay then, let's be off… Time waits for no man," Fedora added with a cheeky grin.

CHAPTER TWELVE:

THE 30-SECOND GOAL

<u>Saturday. 20th April 1895. 3.05pm.</u>

"Play up Aston Villa, avenge 1892," Andy read the words from a huge chocolate brown on white silk banner. It was carried taut between two poles by two ruddy cheeked men with smiles as broad as their arms. Behind the huge flag a large crowd had been assembled and was marching noisily towards the recently opened Crystal Palace Sports Ground in London.

A warm, sunny spring afternoon greeted the travellers on their arrival from Limbo, and despite the cooling breeze the children of the 80's were soon squirming in their rough clothing and peaked caps. And it was just such clothing, rough jackets, scarves tied firmly around necks and the proliferation of cloth caps that showed them that this was not a modern football crowd.

It was 1895 and the supporters of Aston Villa and West Bromwich Albion had poured out of the Midlands in their thousands to watch what was considered by most to be the decider, with both sides having won one Cup Final at the expense of the other in the previous eight years.

"Villa are clear favourites for the game. West Brom are at the bottom of the league," Fedora said, setting the scene. Once again her soft, playful voice was at odds with the gruff masculine image she had constructed for herself back in Limbo. Andy was mesmerised by the movement of her skinny moustache, which bobbed around as she spoke.

Jo eyed the crowd suspiciously and frowned. "What's this game going to be like?" She asked. "Are they all gonna be wearin' shorts down to their knees, them big leather boots and greasy centre parts?"

"Bum 'eads!" Andy blurted out. "Are they all gonna be bum 'eads?" he asked, half shouting. A wisen faced old man with a thick white moustache scowled down at him, and Jo winced and held up a palm in apology.

"Andy don't be rude," she chided behind a fake smile and gritted teeth. "Are they though?"

"Hmm… Oh yes, I suppose they are," Fedora answered. "What we are going to see is not only the first final played at Crystal Palace but also the fastest goal ever scored in a Cup Final."

"Honest?" Jo smiled with honest excitement. "How fast was that?"

"Thirty seconds would you believe!"

"Wowsers. What was the final score?"

"Well if you don't know then I won't spoil it for you, you'll enjoy the game all the more."

"I bet West Brom win," Andy challenged.

"I bet they don't," Jo retorted.

"Bet ye'."

"Go on then smart lad, how much?" Demanded the teenager, holding out her hand.

"Anythin'," the boy said boldly.

"Anything is it? Okay then." Jo thought for a moment, stroking her chin for effect until it came to her. "Your comic! The number one. The Intense Spider-fella."

"*Amazing*... Anyway, get lost!" Andy said, protectively clutching the side of his coat that held his cherished find.

"Come on. You're so sure West Brom will win," Jo taunted, "put your money where your mouth is then."

Andy, the stakes clearly too rich for his blood, quickly tried to find a way out. "Well, what have YOU got to bet with ey? That stupid plastic comb you're alway fiddling with, don't make me laugh."

"I don't need anything," Jo informed him in a superior tone. "I'll win anyway."

"It's nearly 3:30. Come on," said Fedora laughing. "If we don't hurry up we'll miss the first goal."

"Good to see some things don't change," Jo said, happy to let Andy off the hook. "If you go to a midweek game these days, I mean, in my time, you never get in on time. No-one goes before twenty past seven and they don't open all the turnstiles, so it takes ages to get in. I got in at half-time a couple of years ago and Liverpool were already three up and I STILL had to pay full price! AND the ground was half empty. I wasn't half raging, and me Dad was LIVID! He said he was never goin' again. He did though. My Dad says he misses more goals than Trevor Francis." Jo laughed at her own joke, before remembering her audience. "Oh I suppose you won't have seen him, will you? Oh Fed, he was great."

"Well if we miss this goal, we'll keep going back until we get there on time," Fedora announced with a straight face, but the gleam in her eye revealed the humour she intended. As they took their places on the high banks that surrounded the pitch and provided a natural stand in the new stadium, the game started with a roar.

"Gosh, there's still loads outside; they'll miss it," Jo said, herself, wary of not taking her eyes from the golden sun-streaked, green glow of the pitch.

"I'm afraid you're right," Fedora agreed. "Watch." Aston Villa had kicked off with the sun and wind in their faces and immediately lost possession.

"Go on Higgins!" A thick brummie accented voice shouted above the ever increasing crowd.

Higgins however lost the ball to the claret and blue shirted Villa inside left who, under pressure from two West Bromwich defenders, slipped the ball to the outside right. He centred quickly and his inside forward, Chatt, shot at goal. The Albion goalkeeper cleared easily but hit Chatt in the chest with the ball. The crowd let out a collective gasp!

Confusion reigned in the goalmouth with the Villa centre forward Davey prominent. The ball moved back towards the goal where the full back, Horton, perfectly placed to clear the danger, totally missed his kick and the ball bounced into the goal. The crowd erupted into a mix of elated passion, and comic disbelief.

"I hope he doesn't own a pub," screamed Jo amid the celebrations, "or he'd better go and get his windows boarded up now."

"Was that it?!" Andy shouted.

Fedora laughed. "It may not have been spectacular but it was certainly historic. Now shhh! Watch the game."
Villa continued to dominate, their forwards clearly giving them an edge but the only other goal they scored was disallowed.

At half time, as Andy tried from his strained tip toes to count the number of spectators perched in the trees outside, Jo picked Fedora's brain. "Did West Brom get relegated as well as lose the cup then?

"Actually that's a very interesting question. West Brom had lost their last six league games before the final, and because they had lost five-nil at Bolton after their goalkeeper was sent off, they had to win their final game by five clear goals to stay up."

"Who was it against?"

"Sheffield Wednesday."

"And did they do it?"

"Interestingly they scored in the first minute as well. They were four up by half time and won six-nil."

"Go 'way!" Jo was pleased. "That sounds dead excitin'!"

A roar from the now packed crowd indicated the return of the teams to the field.

As they kicked off Jo asked, "Who did go down then? It wasn't Wednesday was it? They'd kill themselves!"

"No, as a matter of fact... It was Liverpool."

"WHAT!!!" Jo screamed before catching herself and shouted, "err... Come on the Villa!"

"I'm afraid so."

"I knew I liked them," Andy chimed in, cheekily.

The game continued to be one-sided, and though no further goals were scored, prolonged cheering by the Villa supporters continued even after the presentation of the Cup.

As they shuffled away from the ground and the thinning crowd dispersed in the South London streets, Jo became thoughtful.

"Was it true? What you said before about going back if we missed the goal, 'cause that means we could go back to 1966 and put the World Cup back."

"I'm afraid not," Fedora replied, scratching an itch next to her spirit gummed moustache. "I was only joking. The danger is that we would be there twice and meet ourselves. I'm not sure what that would do exactly, or even if it's possible, but I wouldn't want to risk it."

Jo sank visibly with the news. Travelling through time and visiting old football matches was fine but she was beginning to feel homesick. The uncertainty was the real killer, not knowing if it was even possible to get home.

The trio strode on in silence, as the last vestiges of the football crowd disappeared. The highs of the match had faded and Jo, trying to fight against her sinking mood, looked over at Andy. The young man, who looked so tiny in his big coat, seemed to be struggling with his own thoughts too. The boy to this point had been like a sponge, soaking up every single sight, smell and drop of information contained in each new environment they visited. Now, with his skinny arms buried deep in his coat pockets, and hat pulled down low he looked like he was actively trying to shut out the world around him. His demeanour worried Jo, it was very un-Andy like. Just as she was about to reach out to him, the MIKE bracelet on Fedora's wrist chirped in what sounded like a fanfare. Fedora stopped walking, and the kids, puzzled, stopped a step later.

"Yes. Yes? Oooh, yes…" she said as MIKE chimed away. Jo thought she sounded like her Mum talking on the phone to her auntie. "Fascinating. Okay, thanks MIKE, excellent work! Cheer up guys," Fedora said, turning to them with something similar to a comforting smile, in spite of the grizzled, masculine makeup. "We may not be able to take the cup back to the exhibition, but I think we can return it some other way."

"Really?!" Jo's eyes lit up. "Andy, did you hear that?"

"Yeah." Andy said flatly, though Jo was too excited to notice.

"Why the change of heart?" She asked Fedora a bit callously.

"Well I've always intended to return you to your own time. I just had to be sure that it WAS your time. If I'd just taken you back you could have ended up in 1986 but in a world you didn't know."

"A parallel world," Jo said, pleased that she was starting to learn the sci-fi lingo..

"Yes, and one in which you may have had no homes or families."

"Big deal," mumbled Andy. His companions heard his downbeat tone, and gave each other a questioning look before continuing.

"So why are you so sure now?"

"Well, remember when you knocked me down in Central Hall?"

"Yeah?" Said Jo suspiciously.

"What do you remember?"

"What? Well I dived at you and knocked you down."

"Anything else?"

"No." She said, but stopped for a moment. "Wait. Yes. Something fell. The two fellas grabbed it and ran."

"Right. The cup you see had an eight sided lid. When you tackled me it fell to the ground, and the thieves ran off with it."

"Yeah, so? Why's that important?" Jo queried.

"Well, in my time the whole trophy was stolen. None of it was recovered. So it CAN'T be my world."

"I don't follow."

"In your world the thieves have sent the top back and asked for a ransom."

"How do you know that?" Jo asked, her freckled nose wrinkling in puzzlement.

"Whilst you two were getting changed I asked MIKE to do some digging, and during the match he sent a probe out into the timestream, back into 1966, the day after the robbery. MIKE gave an affirmative chirp. We need to go and pick up the papers to be sure."

Jo instinctively reached out and gripped Fedora's sleeve. Andy, uncharacteristically quiet, sighed and did the same. Limbo beckoned once again.

CHAPTER THIRTEEN:

DESTINY

<u>Limbo. Everywhere and nowhere, baby.</u>

"It says here that the police are looking for a middle aged man, with a sallow complexion and greased back hair," Jo read.

"Hey, that must be Fed." Andy said, his depressive tone once again replaced with his usual perk.

The two reluctant time travellers were sitting in the Limbo library scouring the array of newspapers their hostess had amassed for them across the techno-mahogany table. Each was placed neatly with a clear gap between, as per instruction from their other host. As they read, the artefacts were ringed by a glowing light as MIKE scanned them into his database with a pleasant hum and subsequent "ping" noise upon completion.

Fedora herself had disappeared to change and left the youngsters to read about the theft they had unwittingly been involved in.

"Urgh, these papers are such a pain," said Andy in exasperation as he struggled to turn over a page, with the broadsheet paper flopping limply over on itself despite his best efforts, "the size of them! Stupid!"

Jo shook her head and let out a laugh at Andy's near farcical handling of the paper, before continuing. "At least there's nothing in here about us, is there MIKE?"

"In all of the periodicals that I have scanned, there have been five mentions of a person resembling Miss Fedora, three that hint at the presence of two other gentlemen, and one rather unusual claim pertaining to an extraterrestrial presence, but zero mentions of two young people involved in the incident."

The kids, who had been expecting a simple affirmative, stared at the table for a moment before shaking their heads and carrying on their train of conversation.

"Who cares anyway? What could they do even if?"

"Yeah, I 'spose you're right. But at least if we put the cup back we won't have messed anything else up," Jo explained.

"Yeah," Andy sighed mournfully, "and then we can go home."

"More importantly, we can go the match!" Jo stood up and danced around the room with a returning sense of joy.

"Yeah, and the Comic Mart."

This brought Jo up short. "Oh no!"

"What d'ye mean no?"

"I'm not going through all that again," Jo announced forcefully, wagging a finger at her companion. "As soon as I get back to Central Hall in *our* 1986, I'm walking out and not looking back. If I never set eyes on that place again it'll be too soon."

"Why? Haven't you liked time travel?"

"A bit. It was great going to the Inter Milan game,

and seeing that other stuff was pretty interesting, but give me Kenny Dalglish and Ian Rush any day!"

"Well, I don't see what's so great about home," Andy said bitterly.

"With a team like yours I'm not surprised," Jo goaded.

"ALL YOU EVER THINK ABOUT IS BLOODY FOOTBALL!" Andy shouted in a shocking flash of anger. Jo reflexively leaned away in surprise. The floodgates opened, and tears sprang to the young man's eyes. He threw the newspaper to the floor, kicked his chair back and marched off to the corner of the room. Jo, startled by her friend's outburst, watched the rise and fall of his shoulders as he sobbed. She carefully placed her own paper onto the table, and walked over. As she approached, Andy tried to compose himself, sniffing and wiping his tear stained cheeks firmly with the bobbled sleeve of his tracksuit top.

"Hey, I'm sorry," she said, placing a hand on his shoulder from behind.

"You keep going on about home like it's this perfect thing. Oh yeah for you it's perfect anyway. What a life you've got. Going the footy with your Dad, getting to go home to your family, school: sound, friends: no worries, clothes: boss. What am I going back to ey? EY?!" He turned to look up to Jo, his eyes red, tears streaming down his blotchy cheeks.

"Another week in the boys home. Another day of patching up tatty clothes and hiding from truancy officers, another night reading stupid kiddy make believe stories and wishing some magic chemicals would splash me, or a stupid radioactive spider would bite me, or, someone would just come and take me away from it all."

He sharply pulled his Spider-man comic from the inside of his jacket and hurled it across the room, it hit one of the book cases, the staples split, and the pages spread out loosely on the floor. Seeing what his anger had done to his prized possession, his legs gave way and he slumped to the floor with his back to a bookcase; he put his head to his knees and stopped trying to stop himself from crying. To Jo's eyes, the lad she knew, the self confident little rogue all of a sudden looked very much like the lonely, outcast, ten year old boy that he really was. She sat down beside him, shoulder to shoulder.

"Andy, I… I'm so sorry. I never really thought about what home actually meant to you, about what it is you're really going back to. This whole thing…" She looked around the room and its seemingly endless shelves of books, "for me it's been a nightmare, i've been half scared out of my mind ever since we got here. But for you, God, it must've felt like all your dreams come true."

Andy sniffed again, and wiped his face with the palms of his hands as he lifted his head to face her. "I can't go back there Jo."

Jo, not normally one for physical affection, put her arm around his shoulder. After a moment, she asked, "but what about your Mum and Dad, what would they say?"

"They wouldn't care, not really. The only thing my mum would miss about me is the benefits cheque, and my Dad, heh," he laughed bitterly, "if he sobers up enough to notice i'm gone, he'll soon find something else to take his moods out on."

Jo's stomach dropped, and she hugged him in closer and even tighter.

"Maybe I'll just stay here with Fedora…"

"What makes you think she'll want to put up with a little rogue like you?" Jo said playfully, trying to lighten the mood.

"Ey!" Andy said in mock annoyance, wiping his face again. "I'm a delight. Better than you anyway!"

Jo chuckled and gave him another playful squeeze. Before she could retort, Fedora; once again in her natural feminine state, arrived back in the room with another pile of books and newspapers. The pair clambered back to their feet. Andy quickly wiped his face again, and Jo gave him a caring smile, they then followed her over to the table.

"Okay," she said in a business-like manner. "I think I've sorted this out. It's clear from the papers that the authorities believe that the whole trophy was stolen intact. Someone was arrested on the Saturday after the cup was taken and it was announced that earlier in the week the eight-sided top piece had been posted to the Football Association headquarters with a ransom note for £15,000."

Andy whistled through his teeth. "Just think how much we could get for the rest," he smirked.

"And then you'd never get to go home," Fedora told him.

Andy looked at Jo and gave her a faint smile. "Sorry, yeah you're right, we need to do this properly."

"The crux of the matter rests on the return of the cup. A report in the Guardian for Monday 28th March tells how the cup was found, and yes it's how you had said previously Jo, by a dog. Its name was Pickles. If we don't return the cup then the future from that moment will be changed, and it won't be your future any more."

Fedora stopped to let that sink in. "We must go to the exact time and place that the trophy was found and make sure it's there for Pickles to find. Then you can go home."

"Great!" Said Jo as a wave of relief rushed through her. But, as she thought about Fedora's plan, she began to feel some concern. Turning to the older woman she gave her fears a voice.

"It will be OUR future though right?" She asked.

"The mission has a 97.1% chance of success." MIKE's disembodied digital voice chimed in. Andy nodded, impressed.

"Mechanical. Information. Kollecting. Enigma, oh no, wait.." he muttered, half to himself.

Jo rolled her eyes and continued, still not totally convinced by Fedora's plan. "Oh, okay. But what will you do?"

"I'll think of something."

"Hang on," Andy spoke up, his mind back on the job at hand. "Why didn't you just do all this before? Go out and get a paper and see what happened?"

"Andy, forget it," Jo admonished him.

"No Jo, it's a good question," Fedora admitted. "Originally I thought that the moment we stole the trophy was the crucial point where your world and mine diverged, you know," she gestured running both her slender hands parallel and then splitting them away from one another, "went their separate ways. However, well MIKE you tell them, i'll go and make us all a drink before we go."

MIKE's rich digital tinged voice filled the air around them again. "Based upon my data calculations, I convinced Miss Fedora that, as the Jules Rimet trophy was stolen in both your world and hers, then the crucial moment could only be at the later point when it was returned, or not returned as the case may be."

"But can Fedora get home if she returns the cup?" Jo was determined not to skip the issue of her hostess' future.

"I believe so. You see, I calculate that your being dragged into our path was what pushed us off course. With you back in your own world we can return to 1966, allow the cup to be stolen and return again to our own time."

"What if the thieves return the cup?"

"Well we figure," Fedora picked up the explanation as she returned, balancing a tray filled with various cups, pots and bottles, "that the only reason the thieves in your time returned the trophy was because they didn't have it."

"Yer wha?" Andy scratched his head, "That makes abar as much sense as… as…"

"Any of this?" Jo offered.

"Yeah. S'pose." Andy shrugged with acceptance.

"Yes it does sound rather daft," said the computer

Andy giggled at MIKE's phrasing. "Aren't you meant to say 'illogical' or something like that?"

"But it is logical Andy," the computer continued. "You see, if they had the whole cup they would not have returned it. They would, rather, try to ransom it for £1 million as they did in our time. The demand would be refused and the cup would never be seen again. Probably melted down."

"However," Fedora again took over, more animated this time, pacing the floor, "we stopped them getting away with all but the top. They make a half hearted attempt to convince people that they have the whole lot by sending the top to the F.A. If we return the cup, their little game is over."

She paused to take a breath, with her back turned to the kids. Her demeanour was buzzing with energy, as she built towards her Eureka moment.

"It would appear that our joint arrival in 1966 was not as haphazard as we first thought. If I had not arrived then the cup would have been stolen, lost forever and football destroyed. If I'd arrived alone I would have stolen the whole trophy and inadvertently destroyed the game I was trying to save." She turned back to face them. "Your arrival, Jo and Andy, ensured the cup was returned and football saved. It was - is - your destiny."

"*Like Luke Skywalker...*" Andy whispered in wide eyed awe.

"So you can defo go back?" Jo asked again, totally ignoring Andy's geekish mutterings. Fedora nodded reassuringly, and Jo felt her shoulders unknot and her stomach settle.

"Honestly. Now, come on you two, drink up, your destiny awaits!"

"Destiny?" Andy downed his cup of tea. "Piece of cake mate."

CHAPTER FOURTEEN:

A PIECE OF CAKE

Sunday. 27th March 1966. 7:30pm.

"A piece of cake you said!" Jo's anger was evident as she searched her pockets for her comb.

"Well how was I s'posed to know?" Andy was no more pleased than his friend. "I thought stupid MIKE knew everythin'. Wait 'til I see him," he said clenching teeth and fists.

"I'm sorry," Fedora said abjectly as she plonked her slight frame down beside her two young friends on the edge of a kerb in a South London street. "Beulah Hill, Norwood. The report didn't say any more."

Night had recently fallen and a pale three-quarter moon and some hazy star clusters added little to the local street lighting. Though in nearby gardens, unseen, daffodils had bloomed, there was a winter chill still lingering in the air. A noise of distant traffic came intermittently to their ears.

"We need the number," Jo said, dejection written clearly on her face. "Just the number of the silly house."

"As I recall the report wasn't even clear about whose

house it was," Fedora said, quite unsure of what to do.

"I thought it was Pickles' house," Jo suggested.

"Pickles!" Andy laughed. "We must be looking for a dog house then." His joke had no effect on his disconsolate friends.

"Yeah, well that's where I'll be if I don't meet my Dad outside White Hart Lane at two," Jo moaned.

"Southampton!" Andy laughed callously. "From what MIKE says, you might not even have a Dad if we don't get this cup back."

The MIKE interface on Fedora's bracelet responded with a puzzled "twooo" sound. Andy turned to Fedora. "Look, can't we just dump it? I mean if this is our destiny won't Pickles just find it anyway?"

"Hmm… It's an interesting idea but a bit risky, don't you think?" She replied.

"We don't have much else though do we?" Jo's anguish leaked out in her words.

"I couldn't guarantee history wouldn't be changed if the trophy was found by someone else." Fedora pushed her blonde hair back from her tired face in a gesture of dismay and looked down at the trophy, wrapped in newspaper and twine alongside her. "It could be disastrous. What if they stole it? Heaven forbid. Maybe we should go back to Limbo and do some more research. MIKE let out a disconsolate sounding "bloop". Fedora sighed.

As they sat contemplating the seemingly insoluble problem, a noise from behind grabbed their attention; the sound of a door opening and people's voices.

"Quick, this might be it," Fedora regained her composure first. "Andy, get the trophy into the bottom of that garden by the gate! Go! Go!"

The boy, for all his own intentions, knew the urgency of the situation. He grabbed the newspaper-covered bundle and ran, stooped over, towards the gateway directly behind them.

Andy, never one to miss the chance to get his knees muddy, pushed open the gate and front rolled into the garden. Dropping the bundle on the grass as he completed the manoeuvre, he scrambled under the overgrown privet hedge that bordered the next garden, and pushed himself upwards into the foliage.

A few branches cracked noisily and a couple of twigs stuck in his back, scratching the skin, but, squirming from side to side he managed to lodge himself fairly comfortably into the bush, able to see the package clearly, but deep enough to remain hidden in the gloom.

The dark, earthy smell of soil, grass and leaves filtered into his nostrils, reminding him of autumn games of hide and seek, and kick the can. The boy held his breath and felt his heart banging against his constricted chest.

A rustling in the grass grabbed his attention and heard the heavy panting of a big, excited dog sniffing its way along the lawn towards him.

"Rags!" A male voice roared with a mild southern twang. "Here boy. I've forgotten my keys. Here!"

"*Rags?*" Mumbled Andy to himself. "Rags? That's not right... Oh, no!" He said out loud as realisation dawned on him. "It's the wrong Dog!"

In his agitation, he fell out of the bush flat onto his face. As he lifted his head, blowing loose soil from his lips he found himself staring into the face of a big, shaggy haired old English Sheepdog. Its small pink eyes blinked questioningly at him from beneath a mass of fringe, and a big red tongue lolled out of the side of its mouth. Andy was so close he could see bubbles of saliva around its jaws, and as the dog panted vigorously, a flash of yellow teeth sent his pounding heart into a frenzied attack on his rib cage. The dog's tail wagged wildly.

Steeling himself, Andy glanced past the dog and saw in the distance its master with his back turned, knocking at the front door of the house. Keeping his head perfectly still, Andy moved his eyes to the left and sighted the bundle he had dropped. Any second now the man would turn back to check on the dog and see him! All would be lost.

Jo, who had made it to the gate scant seconds after Andy watched on through a gap in the fence, feeling like their moment of triumph was close at hand. Until she followed the big shaggy dog's gaze and saw Andy, partially obscured by the hedge, with a look of abject panic on his face.

"Andy!" She hissed. "Andy! What's up?"

She was too far away to hear his response instead focussing on trying to read her friends lips and frenzied hand signals.

"It's the wrong… log?" She mouthed, wrinkling her nose in confusion. "Well that's just nonsense. Oh… Wait. Oh no!" She said as comprehension dawned on her, and terror gripped her heart. "It's the wrong dog!"

Her eyes darted to the back of the house, and the distracted owner. Jo knew that the countdown clock to failure was ticking. She imagined her Dad, her uncle, her Mum and all her stupid warnings, she imagined Kenny Dalglish, broken and retired, never getting his chance to shine on the biggest stage.

"No, that can't happen, it won't."

Jo, steeled by determination and a rush of adrenaline

sprinted along the pavement, put her right hand on the gate top, and in one fluid motion, gracefully leapt over. She landed silently into a cat-like crouch on the other side, touching her hand to the bundled trophy. She was about to vault back over the gate when another noise alerted her.

"Pickles! Pickles! Don't run off!" came the faint voice.

Jo froze in the open. She looked across the garden at Andy under the bush, behind the, now it was up close, HUGE shaggy dog. Andy had clearly heard the call too, he frantically gestured for her to come to him.

"Come on!" He mouthed, with his soil stained face.

A jangle of keys at the back door of the house set her nerves on edge again.

"Ahhh, there we go! Come on Rags! Where are ya Raggsy?" The house owner said as he finally gained entry.

Time had run out. Jo played the scenario out in her head as time slowed to a crawl, the gap from her to Andy was just too great, she could make it back to the gate, but if she took the trophy she might miss her window to get it to Pickles in the neighbouring garden. Her eyes drifted back down to the trophy, the thick newspaper wrapping rounding off its pointed edges, its back print barely legible in the moonlight. If she left it there, the wrong dog would have it, and therefore the wrong owner, even if he handed it in, history would be changed and who knew what fresh disasters that might unlock? Then it hit her. Jo quickly rose to her feet, gauged the angle and distance and felt the faint breeze on her cheek. Pulling back her right foot, she cushion-passed the bundle with her instep, and as it left her, immediately sprang back over the gate.

Andy, eyes wider than the Mersey tunnel, watched on as his friend disappeared over the gate and the bundle bobbled its way across the turf, past the wagging tail of Rags, into the soil border in front of him and nestled safely into his chest. He cradled it in with a faint "oof" sound and gripped it tightly in place.

    Jo landed on the other side, heard Andy's quiet impact and pumped her fist in celebration. Fedora met her there and helped her to her feet. The Woman gave her a questioning look.

    "Wrong dog. Next door. Come on!" Jo said for both brevity and lack of breath. The pair scrambled along the road searching for a vantage point to see what happened next.

    Rags the dog, startled by the flying bundle, leapt backwards in fear, and landed with its legs slightly splayed. Its tail, up until now busy in a propeller-like motion, stuttered like a helicopter blade running out of fuel, and the beast bolted over to his owner.

    "Raggsy, there's a good boy, come on then let's get a spot a' supper ey?"

    Andy, pulse racing, clutched the bundle to his chest as though it were the only thing keeping his heart from leaping out of his body. He wanted, needed, a minute to compose himself, but there was no time to waste, as he heard footsteps approaching. Without hesitation, he began to squirm his way backwards through the hedge. His jacket snagged and as he pulled he heard it rip. Still he pushed onwards. He felt a sharp pain on his cheek and knew the wetness that followed was blood flowing down his face. He pushed on further. To stop meant disaster.

    Fortunately there was no fence on the other side of the privet and he painfully edged himself through into the next well-tended garden.

Andy looked up, the blood now dripping from his jawline. The black and white face of another, smaller dog greeted him with the same alert, questioning expression he had just seen on Rags. Andy, adrenaline pumping, looked it boldly in the eye.

"I'm about to make you famous Pickles." He grimaced.

The dog tilted its head to the other side.

"So be a good dog. There's a boy. Here, fetch!" The boy threw the newspaper-covered trophy in a shallow arc towards the garden path, and with the footsteps getting closer, rolled back into the hedge as the dog took off after it.

He watched as the man approached. Pickles was sniffing away at the package.

"What's this then," said the man, his fresh shaven face obscured by the dim light, "the Maltese Falcon?" He chuckled to himself and tore at the newspaper.

"What on earth?" He ripped paper from the other end to reveal a glint of gold. "Blimey!" He said. He looked around the garden. Andy, now back in the foliage, held his breath as the man's eyes scanned over his location. The sound of his own heartbeat filled his senses. From behind a broken fence panel at the bottom of the garden, Jo and Fedora too held their collective breath and gripped each other's hand tightly.

The man shrugged, turned around and carried the Jules Rimet Trophy back into the house, with Pickles trotting along proudly behind him.

Back in Rags' garden, Andy rolled out of the soil and lay panting on the grass. He had felt exhilarated and alive with the adrenaline pumping through his veins, but now the escapade was over and he relaxed with his back stretched out on the lawn in the moonlight. A feeling of overwhelming tiredness overcame him and he thought about snuggling down as though it were his own bed. Through the fatigue a touch of sadness hit him; whereas Jo was desperate to get back to her normal life, the thought of returning to his was far less appealing. Andy lay there and his mind hazily drifted back across their adventures, the excitement, the thrill, the escape. The only thing he'd miss from home was his comic collection, and right now, his bed.

"Andy! Get up!" A familiar voice said, melting into his reverie.

" Just five more minutes Mum," Andy said woozily.

"Mum! I'll Mum you you little villain, get up!"

"Wha'? Oh!" Andy snapped back to the cool air, damp grass and Jo's face playfully smiling down at him. "I must've dozed off."

"Dozed off! The fate of the world hanging in the balance, and you've decided to have a little kip in some random's garden! Oh, you're cut!" Jo said, her feigned anger replaced by genuine concern as she saw the congealed blood stain across his face and shirt neck.

The lad put his hand up to feel the wound and winced a little, before squaring up his shoulders and shrugging it off. "Nah it's sound yer know, just a scratch."

Jo smiled at her young companion's display of bravado.

Fedora entered the garden, a beaming smile on her delicate features. "Mission accomplished?" She asked.

"Pickles, the wonder dog has saved the day once again," he said, rubbing his back gingerly as Jo hoisted him to his feet.

"Oh Andy, that's great work, but we know who the real heroes are today," Fedora said, and pulled her two young friends in, putting an arm over each of their shoulders. Andy and Jo, with palpable relief, relaxed into her grip.

"Fedora?" Andy asked as they walked back through the garden gate onto the street.

"Yes?"

"Can you transport large objects through time?"

"I suppose so. How large are you talking?"

"Oh, I don't know, about the size of a bed?"

Fedora laughed as she activated her bracelet, and the world swooshed to black around them.

World Cup found by a dog

By OWEN SUMMERS

THE World Cup was found last night in the garden of a house in Beulah Hill, Norwood, by a man taking his dog for a walk.

Police had been making an intensive hunt for the cup in South-East London since it vanished a week yesterday from Central Hall, West-minster.

Comment
The roads to riches

CHAPTER FIFTEEN:

A MESSAGE FROM THE PAST

<u>Limbo. The world of betwixt and between.</u>

"We did it!" Jo shouted, jumping around the brightly lit library, twisting and turning before punching the air like a goal scoring forward. "WE DID ITTTTT!!!"
She threw her arms around her older companion and the two women hugged as they bounced up and down on the spot.
Andy ignored their celebrations and, sitting at the techno-table, began to look through the newspaper account of the adventure he had just engineered. He knew there was no mention of him in the report, how could there be? But it was annoying to play such a major part in history and get no recognition.
He pushed that paper aside and picked up an earlier one and began to read the account of the original theft.
"So now we can go home," Jo said breathlessly. "That's right isn't it MIKE?"
"Yes," agreed the computer voice, "and with you home we should be able to go back to 1966 and pick up our own

time-line again."

Jo stopped dancing, "But what about your dream Fedora, of getting football going again in your world?" She'd been so lost in her own win that she'd forgotten all about her new friends' plight.

Fedora rested her hand on the table, she frowned and shrugged her shoulders. "I don't know." A look of tiredness swept over her youthful features.

"Well, at least you've SEEN some real football now," Jo said, trying to be cheerful.

"Yes, but in some ways that makes it worse. The only top class football I can see takes place before 1966, and that in itself could be fraught with trouble. What if I accidentally take a ticket that was supposed to go to someone who, historically speaking, needed to be at that game? What if I end up dragging other people back with me again, or inadvertently impact a major event and end up in a similar bind again? No," she said with her resolve returning, "I've got to find a different way to get it off the ground again in my own time. But, without that cup…" Her voice trailed off, and shook her head and her shoulders slumped again.

"You're not thinking of trying to steal it again are you?" Jo asked, her brow furrowed in concern.

"No, no I wouldn't take the chance. It should have been perfect, stolen and never found. MIKE and I were convinced, weren't we?"

"Yes," the computer affirmed, "stolen and never found. It was perfect."

The words hung awkwardly in the air. Fedora looked at the floor, Jo became very aware of how loud she was breathing, and how selfish she'd been to celebrate so callously.

"Never mind," Fedora consoled herself, "at least you will get back safely, and I hope that despite your initial fears you have enjoyed yourselves. I just wish I could…"

"Why don't you just steal the F.A Cup?" Andy interrupted.

The two girls stopped, looked at each other and turned to face their little companion. Even MIKE's silence seemed significant.

"What are you talking about?" Jo demanded. "You're stealing mad you!"

"MIKE?" Andy asked to the room.

"Yes, Andy?"

"We saw the F.A Cup being paraded around by Liverpool in 1965 didn't we?"

"Yes."

"What's this about?" A puzzled Fedora tried to interrupt.

"And we saw Aston Villa win the cup in 1895, didn't we?"

"Yes."

"Now MIKE, was that the same cup?"

"No."

"What!?" Jo and Fedora cried in unison.

"Tell them MIKE." Andy sat himself on the edge of the table and swung his legs nonchalantly back and forth.

"Certainly Andy. It's very simple. In September 1895, are you sure you didn't already know this Miss Fedora?" The computer broke off.

"What? No, get on with it MIKE!" Fedora urged.

"In September 1895 Aston Villa put the F.A. Cup on display in the shop window of William Shillcock, a shoemaker.

It was stolen on the night of Wednesday 11th of September and never recovered. The trophy was insured for £200, though only worth in the region of £50. It was eventually replaced by a local silversmith. Aston Villa's first international player, Howard Vaughton was a…"

"MIKE!!! Why didn't you tell me???" Fedora shouted, cutting MIKE's factfile short.

MIKE paused for a moment, and the three friends stared up at the ceiling waiting for his response.

"You never asked," MIKE finally replied matter of factly. "Besides," he continued in a much more conversational tone, "your knowledge of 1895 was so vast, I just assumed that you knew. I would also point out that we both agreed that the theft of the World Cup in 1966 was the significant event we had to use. Adding an alternative seemed… an ineffective use of time."

"Well we were wrong," Fedora confessed, "our intervention was nearly disastrous. Maybe after all we should steer clear of significant events. Too risky." She paused for a moment, deep in thought. Jo and Andy waited and watched. A playful smile grew across Fedora's face. "Then again, 1895 might just fit the bill."

Seeing the gleam return to her friend's eye, Jo couldn't help but smile as well. She turned to Andy, "How come you know so much anyway? Don't tell me you read THAT in a comic too?"

"No, I read it in this."

He held up a copy of 'The Guardian' newspaper he had been reading and pointed to a small advert on the back page. Jo snatched it unceremoniously out of his hands and put it down on the techno-table. Andy traced around the section in question with his fingertip, and it coalesced into semi-transparent light in the air above. It was a copy of a reward notice used to illustrate an article about the theft of the World Cup, which listed other trophies that had been stolen. The advert announced that a reward of £10 was being offered for the safe return of the English Football Association Cup which had been stolen on the 11th of September 1895.

"Look Jo," Fedora said kindly, "I understand what an ordeal this had been, I can take you both home before I go back to 1895, you don't need to come."

"Hey! I wanna come!" Andy announced fiercely. "You probably couldn't do it without me anyway." He said, confidently folding his arms.

"Are you sure you don't want to go back to your father?" Fedora asked.

"Why? It's not like he's going anywhere. We've got all the time in the world right?" Jo replied, also crossing her arms.

"That is indeed correct," MIKE interjected, "unless he also gets drawn into a parallel timeline, when of course…"

"MIKE!!!" All three shouted in exasperation.

"Now, now," Fedora said, trying to calm the situation. "Jo, you could wait here. We'll be no time at all and Andy would be good company for me."

"Good company? Please. If I'm not there, who's going to keep this little villain in check?" She tousled Andy's short bristled hair playfully.

"Ey! Gerroff!" Andy remonstrated.

"Besides, he's my responsibility. I'd better come too."

"Fine," Fedora said with a kindly smile, "I'm really glad to have your help." She winked at Andy, who smiled back proudly in return. "MIKE, what are our chances of success?"

"Processing…" MIKE replied. "The cup was stolen and never found. If you take it before the thieves then the effects will be the same. The cup will be replaced by the insurance company and football will continue to develop as we know it until 1966."

"Good," Fedora nodded in confirmation.

"I must also point out that there may not be any thieves, apart from those in this room."

"Ey! Who are you callin' thieves?" Andy said defensively.

"Well, in point of fact all three of you. To clarify, it is entirely possible that Fedora and yourselves did steal the cup in 1895, always did and always will. You therefore have to steal it to maintain the predetermined flow of time. It is your destiny."

"My head hurts," Jo said with a squint.

"Wow," Andy said in awe. "So, you mean that I actually HAVE to steal something?"

"Indeed," MIKE confirmed.

"Souuunnnnd!" Andy marvelled and rubbed his hands together.

"He's been in training for this his whole life" Jo said to Fedora and poked Andy in the ribs. All three laughed.

"Yeah, I can just see the police now - sorry officer I 'ad to nick it, it was me destiny, ha ha ha ha!"

"So, last chance to back out. Are we in?" Fedora looked at the faces of her young friends and saw in them a steely resolve.

"Yeah man!" Andy shouted.

"Jo?"

"Let's go and save football."

JOHN. J MACHIN

CHAPTER SIXTEEN:

THE FOOTBALL ASSOCIATION CHALLENGE CUP

<u>Wednesday. 11th September 1895. 8:55pm.</u>

It was a dark, September evening and the dappled pavement bore witness to the most recent of the showers that continued to fall intermittently from the cloudy Birmingham sky.

Small puddles of water flickered and shone in the gas light emitted from a row of shops and a line of street lamps. The three time travellers, in flat caps and huddled inside dark, warm overcoats, looked around for some sign that they had arrived in Newtown Row.

"What are we looking for again?" Andy asked and held his hands over his ears as a coach and horses crashed past with a noise like rolling thunder, creaking and roaring its way into the distance. "Blimey, I thought traffic was supposed to be noisy in our time."

"What?!" He roared as Fedora's attempt to answer his earlier question was drowned in the noise.

"Number 73, Newtown Row," Fedora, once again in masculine mode, shouted. "William…"

"Shillcock, boot and shoe manufacturer," Jo, a short distance away completed the announcement, reading the sign above a single storey shop that jutted out from the main building. "Football Outfitter," she read from a sign even higher up on the back wall.

Fedora and Andy splashed through the gathered puddles to join her outside the double-fronted store and gazed into the glass frontage.

Displayed prominently in the centre of one of the two windows was the F.A. Cup, bedecked in claret and blue ribbons. Underneath, a sign declared its identity and explained that it was on loan from Aston Villa, the proud victors in the local battle for supremacy with West Bromwich Albion.

The three stood, slightly transfixed by its sterling majesty. The most famous trophy in England, tantalisingly close.

Jo turned to the others. "Spot on." They nodded in return, a gesture of resolve in the task ahead. Jo bit her bottom lip and searched in vain for her comb. A thrill of fear rushed through her veins and a glow of anticipation lit up her cheeks against the cold.

At that moment a panel was pulled back behind the trophy and the top half of a middle-aged man in a grimy, off-white apron appeared. The three all jumped back with shock, and Andy pulled the peak of his cap further down over his face and hunched his shoulders up to hide his features still further.

The man took no notice of the window shoppers but with practised skill doused the gas lamp glow that had highlighted the ornate silver cup and, pulling back the shutter, left it in darkness.

The gang looked at each other once again and saw each other's faces disappear in the gloom as another interior light was extinguished in the shop.

"Quickly," Fedora beckoned and ushered them to the side of the building.

They listened and heard the shop door being opened and then closed with a ringing of chimes. The rattle of keys indicated that the building was being locked up for the night. They looked on as the shopkeeper turned his collar up and walked away, whistling tunelessly and spinning his keys around his finger as he went.

Somewhere in the distance a church bell chimed the hour. Their breath came hard.

"We'd best wait a few minutes to make sure he doesn't come back for somethin'" Andy suggested with the straightforward attitude of one who'd being caught in the act before.

"This isn't right," Jo said, gripping Fedora's arm. Her moral compass had been spinning wildly since encountering the shop owner. Their intended crime was no longer a faceless one.

"What about the fella? He's going to end up in trouble, anyway stealing is just… wrong."

"Arr yer big softy!" Andy taunted.

"Stop it Andy," Fedora ordered. "It takes more courage to say no in situations like this than to just go along because your friends want you to. If you had shown such courage in the past your life wouldn't be in the mess it is now."

Andy recoiled as if he had been slapped across the face.

"*Fedora!*" Jo said in shock.

"What!" He shouted. "Oh sound yeah, easy for you to

say!" Emotion made his tongue thicken in his mouth and made speech difficult, the blood in his veins ran hot. Tears began to glisten in his eyes. "It's alright for you though ey? Stealing's just a game to you isn't it? You try saying no to your mum and dad. Who helps you then eh? 'Oh Andy, be a good boy'" he mimed, spitting the words out as though they tasted of bitter ashes, "' just stop robbin' and you can go home.' Yeah, well great! They don't say what to do if it's your so-called parents who are the ones that make you steal, do they though?" Andy let out an angry sob.

"Oh Andy," Fedora said sadly. Jo just stood with her mouth open, lost for words.

"Oh Andy nothing!" The boy shouted, tearing off his flat cap and throwing it venomously to the floor where it landed in a a puddle at their feet. Before the water had a chance to soak in, Andy spun on his heel and sped across the road and into the night.

"Andy no!" Jo shouted after him and gave chase, but by the time she reached the other side of the road the splashing sound of his footsteps had faded into the darkness.

"We've got to find him," Fedora told Jo urgently. But the teenager was still in shock from the confrontation. She knew that Andy had been on the edge, but she had never expected Fedora to be the one to set him off. Finally her own anger boiled up.

"What the hell were you thinking? Like he hasn't been through enough! God, how could they do that to him?" Jo's anger trailed off, replaced by awful visions of Andy's life back home. "I mean I've heard stories about it, parents using their kids to steal while they're too young to go to prison, but I never… God…"

Fedora grabbed Jo by the shoulders, shaking her out of her trance.

"Listen. I'm sorry but we don't have time to go into it right now, we need to find him. We can worry about the rest later. If he gets lost in this time the repercussions could be dire. Heaven knows what harm will be done or what harm will come to Andy. There are far more people to exploit him here than at home. You've got to help me."

"Sure, sure" Jo said in a daze, her distress momentarily replaced by the severity of their situation. They were so close to fixing things, she couldn't face it going wrong all over again. "But how are we going to find him?"

"Think. You know him," Fedora stated logically. "What will he do?"

"He'll, urgh, I don't know, break into a shop probably, I don't know, steal something and then come back and erm… pretend nothing's happened, or he'll climb up somewhere an' hide out, god knows."

"Heaven knows the damage he could do. He could take us all into another parallel world," Fedora said in exasperation.

"Oh no, not again!" Jo lamented.

"Come on, let's walk around the area and see if we can spot him, hopefully he hasn't gotten too far."

As they walked, the rain began to fall less intermittently. It was a fine drizzle, hardly noticeable, but just occasionally as Jo looked into a passing street light she could see its silver trails hurrying by into the darkness. She pulled her cap more firmly down on her head and was surprised to find it so wet.

Her misery increased in direct proportion to her wetness. She caught a glimpse of Fedora's masculine painted features, fixed in steely focus as they looked up and down the lamp lit Birmingham street. Thoughts cascaded through Jo's mind, few provided her with any comfort; Andy's parents, stealing, stealing the cup, parallel worlds. She envisaged her Dad waiting at the White Hart Lane turnstile in vain, her mother crying alone at home, Andy cold, upset and frightened, lost forever in the wrong century. Jo herself began to feel the same fear. She felt tears boiling up behind her eyes, tears as much of frustration as sadness.

She looked up and noticed that their path had brought them back to the shoe shop. She blinked back the tears, hoping that the rain and the brim of her hat had concealed them. "Now what?"

"I must get the Cup," Fedora announced. "I understand your moral dilemma, stealing is wrong and I don't want you to take any part in it. I should never have gotten you mixed up in all this in the first place. But, we know that the cup WILL be stolen, and I can't afford to take the chance that I am the one who is destined to take it. If I don't, and I am, then I risk changing the whole future."

"I know, I know, and it could also be the thing that relaunches football in your time too," Jo agreed.

"Well it doesn't matter now. First thing's first. I'll get the cup and then we'll concentrate on Andy."

"No you won't."

"Won't what?"

"You won't steal the cup."

"Why?"

Jo closed her eyes, sighed and pointed at the window.

"'Cause it's already been stolen!"

"What??" Fedora flew past her young friend and

pressed her moustachioed face up against the glass. Even in the darkness it was clear that the trophy had gone. The shutter behind was gaping open.

"Oh no, not again!" Fedora cried, and turning her back to the window, slid slowly down the glass and slumped dejectedly on the wet pavement. "That's it, it's all over."

Jo watched the disturbed droplets of rain that ran erratically across the window pane where Fedora's coat had wiped against it. Her emotions were jumbled. She no longer knew what she thought or felt, but she knew she wanted to see Andy, wanted to hear his voice and his jokes. He was her only connection with home, her own time, her own city. That little rogue was her best friend.

"I'll murder him," she muttered sadly.

"Oh right! That's the thanks I get then is it?" Andy's voice sounded from above them.

Jo glanced up as Fedora shot to her feet in surprise. Andy sat on the edge of the shop sign on the roof, cradling the large silver cup in his lap like it was a teddy bear.

Jo's eyes widened and her jaw dropped in disbelief. Andy gave her a playful smile and swung his legs casually.

Jo, clicking back into big sister mode snapped at him, "Get down from there before someone sees you! I thought you said you'd given up stealing!" She hissed.

"But officer," he said, springing to his feet to balance precariously in a low crouch, "I didn't steal anything, THIS IS MY DES-TIN-Y!" Andy said, deepening his voice for dramatic effect like the narrator of an American radio drama, and gestured.

"Andy!" Fedora warned, but the boy was on a roll.

"DES-TIN-Y, DES-TIN-Y!" He chanted, and gripped

both handles of the trophy, skipped back to balance on the roof's edge and, raising his arms, held the gleaming cup up to the night sky for all the world to see, like the winning captain of the Cup Final. He mock cheered himself.

"There's only one Andy Bellew, ONE ANDY BELLLLEWWW!!" she sang.

Jo and Fedora couldn't help but give in to their friend's infectious enthusiasm. They clapped and cheered along with him, Fedora shook her head, looked at the floor and smiled.

"Here, catch!" Andy said, and tossed the cup down to Jo, whose blood ran cold with terror as she watched it spiral down towards her. She grabbed it firmly out of air and cradled it to her chest. It's cold metal pressed under her chin, the smell of polish filling her nostrils. She looked down at it and let out a sigh of relief so deep it threatened to empty her bones.

"Wow," she exclaimed as she examined the most famous trophy in English football with starry eyes. "It's amazing."

Andy hopped down cooly from the roof and landed awkwardly, with an audible "ooof". He gave Jo a cheeky grin.

"Come now, we must leave before someone sees us," Fedora reminded them.

"Go on." Andy said to Jo, nudging her in the ribs. "You know you want to," he said with a wink.

Jo, trophy grasped in both hands, glanced over at Fedora, whose expression softened. "Go for it." She smiled..

Jo swallowed hard and took a deep breath. Switching her grip on the cup she wiped her palms on the back of her coat.

"And your winning captain, for Liverpool FC…" Andy said in his best announcer voice, "a player even better than

Kenny Dalglish, the one, the only, Miss Jo Johnson!"
He and Fedora broke into a cheer and Jo tightened her grip and pushed the Cup up high above her head. A smile exploded across Jo's face as the rain came down. Andy and Fedora danced around her in celebration, and though it had come to them through ill-gotten means, Jo struggled to believe that winning the Cup Final itself could feel much better.

CHAPTER SEVENTEEN:

BACK TO THE PRESENT

<u>Limbo. Between the sofa cushions of the multiverse.</u>

    Back in the changing room of Limbo, Jo towel dried her hair. Once again she was back in her usual attire of jeans, trainers and beloved black and purple tracksuit top. The clothes felt like a second skin by comparison to the heavy itchy garments of the past. She pulled out her comb from her jacket pocket, looked at it as though seeing it for the first time, smiled and began to brush the knots from her hair. A deep fatigue threatened to overtake her, as the adrenaline of their adventures and the caffeine from countless cups of tea finally began to recede.

    When she was ready, she gave herself one last check in the mirror wall, tucked away her comb, picked up a flat, paper wrapped package from the metal table and headed back to the library.

    "So you gained entry via the roof?" she heard MIKE ask as she opened the door.

    "Yeah." Replied Andy, who was sat with his feet up on the techno-table. He too was back in his usual clothes and freshly showered. He caught Fedora eyeing his dirty trainers and quickly put them down on the floor with an apologetic wince. "It was made of some kind of metal but it wasn't very strong."

"Zinc, I think," MIKE said, managing to sound pleased with his rhyme.

"How do you know that?" Fedora broke in.

"That fact is contained within the report." The computer replied.

"What report?"

"The published report in the Times newspaper." MIKE said matter of factly.

"You mean you knew how to get in the whole time and you never said? Why? No," Fedora stopped herself. "I know, I know, I never asked…" She sighed.

"*Zinc, I think*" MIKE said again, playing with the rhyme.

The trio laughed. Though the mood in the room was as relaxed as Jo had experienced since first arriving in Limbo, one more elephant remained in the room. Its looming mass filled the silence until Jo finally decided to push on.

"Andy, is it true? She asked tentatively. "What you said about your mum and dad, I mean?"

"It doesn't matter, take no notice," Andy said, shifting uncomfortably in his seat, his body betraying his casual attempt to brush off the question.

"I won't," she said firmly, sitting down in front of him. "Tell me. The abuse. The stealing. Is it true?"

Andy looked down at his battered trainers. "Yes. Okay? Now leave it."

"No," Jo pressed on. "Why?"

"Why what?"

"Don't be funny, you know what I mean."

Fedora had finished filing away a book on a nearby shelf and came to perch on the table next to Jo.

"Look," he sighed, and faced up at his friends. His usual playful demeanour was gone, he wore the cold, emotionless face of a child who had grown up with adult burdens. "Mum and Dad 'ad me young, like really young. They never really knew what to do with me, until one day, when we were goin' round the shops I accidentally pulled some clothes into me buggy and the security guard never stopped us when we left. It gave me Mam an idea. You can't be done, can't get locked up, before you're ten y'see. So I was made to steal. Me Dad's not working, remember." Andy made the excuse on autopilot without conviction. "If they were caught they'd go to prison, if I was caught it didn't matter."

"But you got taken away!" Jo shouted.

"Well by the time I was ten, the busies, *the police*, were out to get me and well, by then," he sighed, "by then I just couldn't stop." He let his gaze fall back to his feet.

Jo moaned. "Disgusting."

"The Police?" Andy smirked.

"Don't be funny, you know who I mean."

"Yeah, some people just shouldn't have kids…" he whispered and the room fell silent again.

"Anyway," the boy announced with a striking amount of conviction. "I'm not going back."

"You what??" Jo said, stunned.

"I'm staying here. I almost decided to stay in 1895 but I knew you two would never be able to get the cup without me."

"Fedora!" Jo implored, "sort 'im out will you? This is

crazy! Tell 'im he's got to go back."

"Well," the blonde woman said, it was her turn to shift uncomfortably, "it actually doesn't make too much difference to me. I'd love the company and I'm sure that MIKE could manufacture the necessary documents needed to come to my time. Besides, he doesn't have a lot to go back to does he?"

"But surely that would destroy him or wreck the space time universe or something?" Jo pleaded.

"Well, no not really. He'd be jumping into my world and while it would alter that future, we're already looking to do that by re-introducing the F.A Cup. I guess it would only really have a significant impact if he was destined to become a great important figure in your world, and with the greatest of respect," She looked at Andy who was fiddling mindlessly with the broken zipper on his jacket, "that seems highly unlikely."

Andy looked up and gave her a dopey smile.

"Fedora!" Jo was flabbergasted at her lack of support. "You can't be serious. You don't want this little twerp hanging around, he's daft and tells bad jokes, and he'll eat you out of house and home, and… and…"

Andy looked at her with a calm resolve on his young face. "I can't go back to that place Jo."

"But i'll talk to them, I'll get my dad to talk to them, I'll…"

"I'm sorry Jo, but they are who they are, they won't let me stop. I'm ten now, and they still don't care what happens to me, just so long as it doesn't happen to them.

"What will I tell my Dad?"

And that was it. Try as she might, the only reason that Jo could muster as to why Andy had to go back with her, was so that she could avoid answering some tricky questions.

And so over thick cut ham sandwiches, scones with fresh cream and strawberry jam, and another pot of tea, the trio concocted their story.

  Andy, ever the rogue, had decided to pickpocket and then ditch Jo on the London Underground to go to the Comic Mart, and that was the last she had seen of him. In time, letters would be sent to both Andy's parents and his case worker, lifting the lid on his homelife, and his plans to make a new life for himself in London. In the envelope of the latter, would be sellotaped the £2 that Andy had "stolen" from Jo, and an apology note for his deception, corroborating her tale and leaving her free from further scrutiny. The relevant authorities in the capital would of course be contacted, but London is a big town, with their own caseload of troubled youngsters to keep track of, Andy would eventually become another forgotten name in an ever-growing pile of similar tales. Would Andy's parents be punished? Maybe, maybe not. It wouldn't matter though, as Andy would be safe.

Once their story was straight, the dregs of their tea had cooled and the last crumbs of sandwich and scone grew stale on the ornate china plates, the time travelling trio stood and embraced. Jo squeezed them extra hard, the memories of their adventure flooding over her like a tidal wave, and as she opened her eyes she saw, over Fedora's shoulder, the cup gleaming on the table.

  "If you ever need a centre forward…" She offered.

  "Don't worry, I'll come and get you," Fedora promised, placing her hand fondly on Jo's shoulder. "Ooh, before you go, I have presents for you both." She said and quickly darted out of the room. She returned moments later with two small packages wrapped neatly in brown paper. The first she handed to Andy who rabidly tore it open to reveal a colourful comic book on the inside.

"Amazing Spider-man number 2!!! YERRRSE!!" he said and hugged it to his chest. A brief look of sadness padded over his features. "Oh, if only i'd not wrecked the number one," he said mournfully.

"Well, about that." Jo said with a sheepish grin as pulled out another similar shaped paper package from inside her jacket and handed it to her friend. Andy, with a puzzled look, opened this one more carefully. Inside, distinctly more creased, and held together with more sticky tape than it had been in 1966, was Andy's copy of Amazing Spider-man number 1. The boy looked up at her with tears in his eyes.

"I was going to give it you back home, I figured even a battered copy was worth more in 1986 than no copy at all," she said.

Andy covered the gap between them like lightning, and gripped Jo with a hug that threatened to crack her ribs.

"EY!" She reacted instinctively, before softening, and hugging him back.

Andy, whose face rustled in the folds of Jo's jacket, said something that sounded like a thank you. Jo beamed and gave him one last squeeze.

"Get off me you little rogue, you'll give me a bad reputation, I can't be seen hugging Evertonians!"

Andy stepped back, sniffed and wiped his eyes with the back of his jacket sleeve.

"What are you worried about, that some of our success might rub off on yer?" He said with a cheeky grin.

"Get lost! A blue nose wouldn't even know what

success looked like if he won a raffle." She hit back, a similarly playful smile on her face belying the bitter sweet emotions she felt.

"And this," Fedora interrupted, "is for you Jo."

Jo peeled back the cellotape and methodically unfolded the paper, to reveal her present, a dark green leather-bound book. She turned it over and read the words on the spine.

"The Time Machine, by H.G Wells."

"It was first published in 1895," Fedora explained. "I thought it would make a nice memento of your adventure and if you are ever in need of money I'm sure it will outsell even Andy's comic."

"Oh no, I would never sell it," Jo declared, protectively cradling the book. "Never. Thank you so much Fedora, it's perfect," she said, and hugged the woman once again.

As Fedora prepared for Jo's trip back, the two youngsters turned quietly to each other.

"I'm so sorry Andy. About your parents I mean."

"It's okay Jo, honest." Andy said, with a maturity beyond his years. "There's nothing back for me there but trouble. I have no-one, not really. Sure people think I'm fun, good for a laugh, and some might think I'm useful, but my family don't love me- they just don't know how to. It's not their fault, it's just who they are. Some people aren't meant to be parents. And as for friends, I don't have any. Not real ones anyway."

"Oh Andy, I'll miss you so much. Just being away from you for that time when you ran off, it made me realise, you do have a real friend in me. Don't ever forget it." The pair hugged one final time, much shorter and more courteously this time.

"Take care you little rogue, don't steal anything I wouldn't," Jo said, giving him a playful punch on the arm.

"Good job you run so fast, because you hit like a girl," he said and pulled a tongue.

Jo pulled one right back and smiled.

"Right, we're all set!" Fedora said. "Shall we?"

Jo nodded, and taking a deep breath stepped towards her friend. She took one last look around Limbo, trying to capture every last detail. "Bye Andy, Bye Fedora, oh.. And bye MIKE!"

"Goodbye Jo. See you soon!" MIKE replied in his warm, clipped computer accent.

"Oooh, MECHANICAL. INTELLECT. KIND. ENERGY," Andy mused.

Jo gave a puzzled smile as she held onto Fedora's wrist, "Getting there mate, needs a little work," she said as the world shifted to black around her.

The cool afternoon air of 1986 surrounded her. Letting her eyes adjust she stepped round the corner onto the High Road, filled with a sea of match goers in stone washed denim jeans, red and white scarves with white Red football shirts peeking through unbuttoned jackets. Off in the distance to her right was White Hart Lane stadium. Without even thinking Jo burst into a sprint, ducking and weaving at pace through the throngs, and didn't stop until she saw her Dad, waiting somewhat impatiently outside the away end. She dove straight into his arms. "Ey! Where the bloody 'ell 'ave you been?"

"Nowhere Dad, sorry I'm late, it's been an afternoon and a half…"

Her Dad, a little taken aback at the affection from his

usually aloof teenage daughter, hugged her back and gave her a kiss on the top of the head.

"Come on, let's get in before it gets packed. Have you seen the team news? Kenny's starting!"

"Really?!" Jo said, hugging in even more tightly at his side, as they made their way to the turnstiles. "*Amazing!*"

TOTTENHAM HOTSPUR
FOOTBALL & ATHLETIC CO. LTD.

F.A. CUP SEMI-FINAL
Southampton v Liverpool

SATURDAY 5th APRIL 1986

KICK-OFF — 3 p.m.

STANDING TICKET
EAST TERRACE LOWER

YOU ARE ADVISED TO BE IN POSITION BY 2.15 p.m.

This ticket is used subject to the rules, regulations and Bye-laws of the Football Association and the Football League Ltd.

THIS PORTION
TO BE
RETAINED

Nº 20123

£5.00
INC. VAT

EPILOGUE:

**Wednesday. 25th February 1987, 7:01pm.
Anfield.**

"James Whittaker and Sons, Funeral Directors," Jo said, quietly smiling to herself. She could still make out the words despite the faded and flaking black and white paint and the burglar alarm box stuck in the middle of it. A small hand-written sign nearby told her that the premises were now used for car repairs.

She skipped off the pavement and made her way past the red brick school to the old police station. A modern plastic sign over the front announced 'CITY OF LIVERPOOL HOUSING DEPARTMENT, HOUSING AID CENTRE, HOUSING IMPROVEMENT OFFICE', but over the red main door the words 'Police Station' were still clearly etched. Higher up, a mask was sculptured with the words 'Liverpool City Police' carved around a City badge.

Jo smiled, remembering the policeman she had seen outside this building just ten months, no, 'just *twenty-two years ago*', she mentally corrected herself.

It was much colder tonight, and though the crowd was

not so large it looked like a big gate all the same. She rubbed her gloved hands together, then the arms of her navy blue duffle coat, and checked, for the tenth time that night, that the big buttons on the front were all fastened. She adjusted the collar to make sure that the red and white scarf tied around her neck was still visible. A teenage girl and a young boy bounced past her, their own red and white scarves around their necks, full of enthusiasm as they headed towards the ground. A picture of Andy, holding the gleaming F.A. Cup aloft in the rain came to her and she smiled. In that moment she had been so happy, they all had. Now it seemed like a fever dream. From deep inside her pocket she pulled out a folded piece of paper and examined the genuinely awful handwriting on it for the thousandth time.

"7PM, LIVERPOOL V SOUTHAMPTON. WHERE WE MET THE BIZZIE."

- Your "Amazing" Friend.

Jo looked at her red and green 'Swatch' watch on her right wrist, 7:03pm. She shook her head and began to pace. The butterflies of excitement starting to be replaced by a familiar level of irritation.

"That boy is the only person in the universe who could have a time machine and still be late." She muttered to herself, smiling weakly at a passerby who had overheard her and given a strange look. "Wonderful," she hissed, looking up at the heavens, "I'll bloody murder 'im."

"Hi Jo"

"Andy!" Jo snapped her eyes open, turned around and

there he was. Half a foot taller, his hair now longer and with a smart side parting. He was dressed in a clean black overcoat and dark jeans, but it was definitely Andy. No greater evidence of this was the battered pair of formerly white trainers on his feet, the scruffs and scrapes nearly as dark as the three black stripes on either side. He caught her looking, shrugged and gave her a sheepish grin.

"Gotta 'ave comfy trainees, you never know when someone's gonna chase yer."

"Look at the size of you! Do they all eat fertiliser in the future then?"

"Ha ha ha! Something like that. Come on let's get in, I know you like to watch the warm ups," he said with the same impish grin, but with a new found confidence behind it.

The pair made their way up to the ground, past the derelict black shell of the St. Simon and St. Jude Church, through the metallic clunk of the Kop turnstiles and, in turn, to the spot they had assumed during the Inter Milan game in 1965. The crowd this time was filling up, and although the game ahead of them was another semi-final, The League Cup this time, the sense of anticipation was far less electric.

"Some view isn't it?" Jo said. "Mad to think that we almost lost it all."

"I don't think I ever got to thank you properly," Andy said unprompted.

Jo, her gaze still fixed on the emerald glow of the field under floodlights replied, "I'm pretty sure my ribs will disagree, you nearly hugged me in half. Anyway, have you seen this?" She handed him the match programme, turned to page 21. It showed a full page advert, and a large picture of the Littlewood's Cup, the trophy Liverpool were about to continue their quest for. She pointed to the paragraph of text near the bottom, which Andy read aloud.

"Essayed in London in 1895 - Britain's oldest major soccer trophy. Huh," he said thoughtfully.

"I guess they've got us to thank for that." Jo turned away from the pitch to look at her friend with a smile.

"Yeah, I guess so," Andy smiled back. "So, you gave me a present, but I never got to give you yours."

Jo, whose attention had drifted back to the pitch, responded off handedly "Present? What present?", and was surprised when Andy pushed another piece of paper into her hand. "What's this?"

"Hope," Andy responded, as the players ran out on the pitch. "See you soon," he added as he pressed a button on his black metallic wrist watch, his voice drowned out as the crowd around Jo erupted at the sight of their heroes spilling out of the tunnel and onto the pitch. Jo came down from her tiptoes amongst the hustle and bustle of the packed Kop crowd to study the neatly folded artefact in her hand. She carefully opened it up, and as she did it revealed itself to be a newspaper front page.

"Andy, what's thi…" she looked to the spot next to her where her friend had been standing, but Andy was nowhere to be seen.

"Andy? ANDY!" She raised her voice to be heard above the din of the crowd. Puzzled, she turned her attention back to the paper in her hand. It was the front page of the Daily Mirror, but something about it seemed off, the red top logo seemed to be in the wrong font, the paper too crisp and white, the picture, of a team of women in white kits lifting a trophy, was in full vibrant colour rather than the usual greyscale. She read the headline and byline underneath.

"History Makers,
It's home! Inspirational women win England's first football title in 56 years."

    Her eyes widened as she looked at the date, Monday August 1st 2022. The crowd around her burst into a rendition of You'll Never Walk Alone, and Jo, normally amongst the first to sing along, missed the opening bars as she searched for meaning in the present she'd been given. "Hope?" she asked quizzically to herself.
    The Anfield crowd reached a crescendo of the song, and Jo felt her spirits lift. "Hope," she muttered again, shook her head with a smile, folded away the paper and joined in for the final chorus.
    "With hope in your heart, and You'll Never Walk Alone, You'll Neeeever Walk Alone! Walk On! Walk On!"

THE END

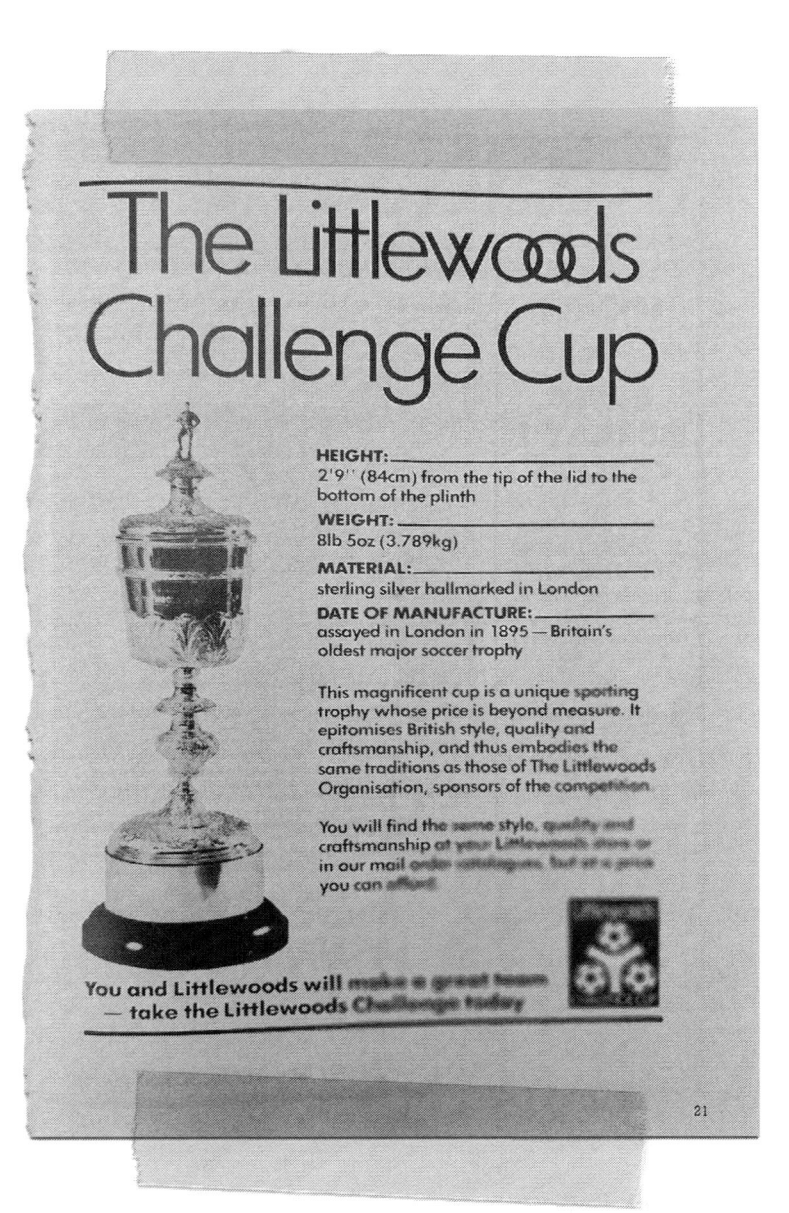

JOHN. J MACHIN

The Littlewoods Challenge Cup

HEIGHT:
2'9" (84cm) from the tip of the lid to the bottom of the plinth
WEIGHT:
8lb 5oz (3.789kg)
MATERIAL:
sterling silver hallmarked in London
DATE OF MANUFACTURE:
assayed in London in 1895 — Britain's oldest major soccer trophy

This magnificent cup is a unique sporting trophy whose price is beyond measure. It epitomises British style, quality and craftsmanship, and thus embodies the same traditions as those of The Littlewoods Organisation, sponsors of the competition.

You will find the same style, quality and craftsmanship at your Littlewoods store or in our mail order catalogues, but at a price you can afford.

You and Littlewoods will make a great team — take the Littlewoods Challenge today

168

THE MAN WHO STOLE THE WORLD CUP

AFTERWORD
By John J. Machin

First off let me clarify that ending. No psychics were harmed in the completion of this novel. Of course it was not written in the 80's as the rest of the book was. Given that a major theme of the book was Jo's anger at the state of women's football in this country at that time, Paul in his capacity as Editor and collaborator felt our knowledge of it's future successful rebirth would add a pleasing finishing touch. We debated it and decided that was the way to go. Was this a good decision? Fortunately you can judge for yourself as you can find the original last chapter in the following appendices. At this point I would like to express my sincere gratitude to Paul for conceiving of a way to get this long forgotten work printed and for finding an audience in the process. Without his hard work, great PR skills and determination it would have remained a memory in a box under my bed. I am also completely blown away by the number of people, over 500, who have pledged their support and enabled the book to be printed. Also all the people who congratulated me in person at the Redmen TV end of season shindig in May 2024.

Being a Liverpool fan can be great at times. YNWA.

THE ORIGINAL ENDING

The pages that follow are scans from the 1987 manuscript of the final chapter.

AFTERWORDS

Chapter 17

Presents

Wednesday. 25th February 1987. 7.00 p.m.

'James Whittaker and Sons, Funeral Directors.' Jo could still make out the words despite the faded and flaking black and white paint and the burglar alarm box stuck in the middle of it. A small hand-written sign nearby told her the premises were now used for car repairs.

She skipped off the pavement and made her way past the red-brick school to the old police station. A modern plastic sign over the front announced 'CITY OF LIVERPOOL HOUSING DEPARTMENT, HOUSING AID CENTRE, HOUSING IMPROVEMENT OFFICE', but over the red main door the words 'Police Station' were still clearly etched. Higher up a mask was sculptured and the words 'Liverpool City Police' carved around a City badge.

Jo smiled remembering the policeman she had seen outside this building just ten months ago, or was it really twenty-two years ago.

It was much colder tonight, she thought, and the crowd was just not so large but it looked like a big gate all the same.

She rubbed her gloved hands together against the cold and began to pace up and down.

A picture of Andy holding the gleaming cup aloft in the rain came to her and she smiled to herself. In that moment she had been so happy and her friends had too. But their celebrations were short lived.

Andy's revelations about his parents cast a dampener on their high spirits and even Mike's enthusiasm for detail had failed to lift them on their return to Limbo.

"So you broke through the roof?" Mike asked.

THE MAN WHO STOLE THE WORLD CUP

"Yes," Andy said quietly, "it was made of some kind of metal but it wasn't very strong."

"Zinc, I think," Mike seemed pleased with the rhyme.

"How do you know that?" Fedora broke in.

"It's in the report."

"What report?"

"In the Times."

"You mean you knew how to get it all the time and you never said....why? No!" Fedora stopped him, "I know, I never asked, don't tell me."

"Zinc I think," Mike played with the rhyme again and Fedora smirked just like Jo might have done.

"Andy, is it true?" Jo asked tentatively. "What you said about your mum and dad, I mean?"

"It doesn't matter, take no notice," Andy brushed the question aside.

"I won't. Tell me. Is it true?"

"Yes. O.K? Now forget it."

"No," Jo pressed on. "Why?"

"Why what?"

"Don't be funny, you know what I mean."

"Because!"

"Andy!!"

"Look. You can't be done before you're ten. So I was made to steal. My dad's not working, remember." Andy made the excuse without conviction. "If I was caught it didn't matter."

"But you got taken away!" Jo shouted.

"Well by the time I was ten, the busies - the police - were out to get me, and..well...I just couldn't stop...honest."

173

AFTERWORDS

Jo moaned. "They need shooting."

"The police?" said Andy smiling.

"Don't be funny, you know who I mean."

"Anyway," the boy announced, "I'm not going back."

"You what?" Jo asked.

"I'm staying here, I almost decided to stay in 1895 but I knew you would never get the cup without me."

"Fedora," Jo implored, "sort him out will ya! Tell him he's got to go back."

"Well," the blonde woman seemed unsure, "it doesn't make any difference to me. I'd love the company and I'm sure Mike could fit him up with all the necessary documents to come to my time. Besides he doesn't have a lot now does he?"

"But surely that would destroy time or something," Jo pleaded.

"Well not really. He'd be jumping into another world and while it would change that world's future - well who's to know. It would only really matter if he was destined to become a great important figure in your world. That seems highly unlikely."

"Fedora!" Jo was flabbergasted at such lack of support. "You can't be serious. You don't want this little twerp hanging around your neck all the time. Besides he'll rob the shirt off your back and eat you out of house and home and.....and.... what will I tell my dad. What will I tell his dad. They all know he's been with me."

"I can't go back to that place," Andy told her.

"But you've stopped stealing."

"Try telling them that," Andy said without specifying who he meant.

"O Andy."

174

THE MAN WHO STOLE THE WORLD CUP

And try as she might she could think of no reason why he should go back except to free her from some tricky questions.

They thought of a story for her to tell of Andy getting lost on the Underground and Jo, with a heavy heart, prepared to take her leave.

She shed her Victorian style clothes and said goodbye and thank you to Mike.

She approached Fedora. The two women looked at each other as they held hands, then spontaneously hugged each other. As Jo opened her eyes she saw, over Fedora's shoulder, the cup gleaming on the table.

"If you ever need a centre forward...." she offered.

"Don't worry, I'll come and get you," Fedora promised. "Before you go I have a present for you." She strode to the centre table and, opening the drawer, took out a couple of packages.

She handed the first to Andy.

"I got this for you in 1965," she announced and passed the thin glossy magazine to the boy.

Andy gasped. "Amazing Fantasy Number 15! Yiiisss! Spidey's first appearance. But how did you know? It's worth a fortune."

"Well, once Mike's on the scent of something it's surprising what information he can dig up."

"O thanks Fedora, thanks Mike." And with that Andy too gave the woman a hug.

"And this is for you." Fedora handed a small book to Jo.

The teenager turned over the leather-bound book and read the words on the spine. 'The Time Machine. H.G. Wells.'

"It was first published in 1895," Fedora explained. "I thought it would make a nice memento of your adventure and if you are ever in need of money I'm sure it will even outsell Andy's comic."

"O I would never sell it," Jo declared. "Never. O thank you," and she hugged the woman again.

As Fedora prepared for Jo's trip back, the two youngsters turned quietly to each other.

"I'm sorry Andy. About your parents I mean."

"It's O.K. There's nothing for me back there. I have no-one. Everyone thinks I'm good fun, good for a laugh, but I don't have any friends. Not real friends."

"O Andy I'll miss you so much. Just being away from you for a while when you ran off, made me realise. Don't ever forget I'm your friend."

Jo looked at her watch as she continued to pace and gave a loud tutting noise. The cold was beginning to get to her feet. Her dad would probably still be in the pub, warm as toast, and she was stuck out here freezing. She hated waiting.

She looked at the houses opposite, trying to spot the differences with 1965. It was a lot easier when you knew you were going to do it. In 1965 it had been difficult to remember what it had been like in her own time, but now she could recall 1965 like it was yesterday.

"This is silly!" she declared looking at her watch again, and then she saw him as he turned the corner and approached her.

"Where have you been, I'm freezing!" she demanded.

"It's a long way from Southport."

"You should have set out earlier."

"It's a community school ye' know, not a holiday camp."

"School for scallies," Jo laughed.

THE MAN WHO STOLE THE WORLD CUP

Andy pulled tongues at her.

"Watch it," Jo threatened as they walked past the derelict black shell of the St. Simon and St. Jude Church and made their way to the ground.

They took up their usual places on the Kop and waited for the kick-off.

"Have you seen this?" Jo pointed to a page in the programme that displayed a large picture of the Littlewood's Cup, the Semi-Final of which they were about to watch. "It says it was 'assayed in London in 1895 - Britain's oldest major soccer trophy'. They have us to thank for that."

"Yes," Andy laughed.

"I wish Fedora was here to see this," Jo said, as it was announced that Kenny Dalglish would be playing. "He hardly ever plays these days."

"Why should she want to see an old man like him?" Andy said smiling.

"Watch it!" Jo warned.

"Do I have to?"

"Andy!"

"Well it's only Kenny Dalglish."

"Andy I'll murder you!"

The End

AFTERWORD TWO
By Paul J. Machin

So there you go! A multi-generational family passion project conceived and executed nearly forty years apart *finally* makes it out into the world! What a wild ride it's been.

This book has been such a core memory of mine since childhood, cropping back into my thoughts on and off across the years. It was first given to me to read by my Dad when I was about 12 years old. My most distinct memory of it though is of being sat in front of our first family PC back in 1998 aged 15, trying to create a cover for it using my (then) rudimentary photoshop skills. It was pretty basic, just one of those famous pictures of Geoff Hurst and the England team lifting the World Cup trophy in '66, but, *sharp intake of breath*, what's this?? The trophy is missing! Yeah, deep stuff, I know.

There are two copies of the original type-writer manuscript in existence, both of which I assumed to be identical. This turned out not to be true in two ways. Firstly, as I sat down to begin the process of digitising the text from the copy in my possession, I discovered to my abject horror that the first page was missing! Had this always been the case, or had it gotten lost on my watch? Probably the latter. Idiot.

The thought of falling at the first possible hurdle because of a lazy past version of myself was absolutely galling. I pressed on regardless, starting from page 2, and hoping that the other copy, the one that was still stashed somewhere at my Dad's house, would have the elusive page. Now, you may not be aware, but in these early stages this project was very much something that I was keeping under wraps. The "Plan" was to get it all typed up and printed, and then give it to my Dad as a present. To ask him to find the other copy for me was a suspect move at best. So I enlisted our Lauren, who still lived with him at the time to be my mole on the inside. Sneak around, secure the package and deliver it unto me. Of course anyone who knows my sister will know that she is funny, creative and a relentless worker. Also if she tells you that she will be somewhere at a certain time, then you add an hour to that time, and THEN start getting ready to meet her.

Anyway, EVENTUALLY I get my hands on this second copy, and yes mercifully there is the missing opening page. Relief. Big fat, palpable relief. What I then discover is the 2nd of the differences. This one has pictures. I'm not sure if you are familiar with the Mandela Effect. The idea that we remember certain things a certain way (often incorrectly), but these memories become foundational somehow moving forward, false memories replace the truth. You see I REMEMBERED these pictures- there's one of the Flyer for Andy's Comic Mart (yes that one, it did actually happen!), a couple of poor quality photocopies of Spider-man covers (the Number One included) and a couple of other bits and pieces too. For the longest time, in that weird way the back of your brain works, I had just attributed it to my childhood memory. Maybe the book had been so descriptive that I just *imagined* seeing them. But no, there they were in the flesh (paper). Where possible I've tried to include these in the pages that follow.

So it turns out that this 2nd version was the actual one that I'd read as a kid, and that at some point, probably when moving out of my mum and dad's house (and in with my future wife Charlie) some time in 2007/8 I'd grabbed the other copy, the pictureless one and taken it with me. I don't have a specific memory of this but it is illustrative of the sense of passion I had to make this thing become a thing. That but also the sense of ownership and responsibility over it. It was a thing. An actual book. Not just some half baked, half written idea, or a bunch of scribbles in a notebook (i've got DOZENS of THOSE). It had a beginning, a middle and an end. It just needed time and attention. So it was in my possession, but it had effectively swapped one loft for another.

The Pandemic had a profound effect on everyone in a variety of ways. For me it was a time of major introspection, and many of those mental rabbit holes were about creative fulfilment and legacy. Football went into lockdown, and with it the central premise behind my company (and first creative baby and main source of income), Redmen TV. No football, no talking points, no insight, no reason for people to watch and/or subscribe. When you own a business that overnight effectively ceases to exist it makes you question if there's another way to earn your money. When you are also approaching your forties, you also tend to question how you are progressing with your life ambitions. There are books I wanted to write, that I had always planned on writing, but life, and other things can often get in the way. And throughout all this a sense of 'what's the point of pouring all my time into writing a book, when there's one already written, sat in my loft gathering dust that just needs typing up and a polish?'. If I wanted to do more with my life, it had to start with 'The Man Who Stole The World Cup'. Nothing else made sense.

So I began. Laptop. Cup of tea. Old paper manuscript (with the missing page). And then? Well life resumed. Football came back, Liverpool won the league, football played behind closed doors, all the staff must be 2 metres apart, Liverpool have an injury crisis, trials of fans back in stadia, another lockdown happens, Liverpool's season crashes, Alisson scores a header, Liverpool save their season, summer break, we buy back our company, Euro 2021, the season starts, my Nephew Taylor is born, fans are back in stadiums, european travel becomes a thing again, going to games home and abroad, Liverpool try to win all four trophies and play in every game in a season, we go to a Champions League Final in Paris and fans nearly die due to inept policing, my wife and I get guns pointed at us by over-zealous French Police, a trophy parade, summer holiday, the season starts again, rinse repeat.

The typing up process goes from serious endeavour to part time obsession to back in a desk drawer.

And then we get it.

Boxing Day 2022. The diagnosis.

We always have Boxing Day at my Mum and Dad's. No one goes the match. We eat my Dad's amazing food and the Machin clan all get together. Family tradition. That's the day I find out that my Mum has been diagnosed with Alzheimer's Dementia. We're getting the spare fold away chairs out of the shed. It's cold, we're wrestling with the rusted padlock, and my Dad drops it into conversation. The truth is that it's not a shock, it's something we've suspected for a year or so. I can tell you now though, having a suspicion, or an inkling, or even a mounted body of evidence? It does sod all to soften the blow of it being actually real. Diagnosis makes speculation concrete. That was the day that this book was truly born.

    It sounds like schmaltz to say it, but I truly believe that you have to make negatives the catalyst for positive change. Of course that's not to say that it made the situation any easier. I would love to say that making this book made it better, that the money it generates could somehow be used on a cure. That's a story I would pay to see brought to life. No, none of that, life goes on. It has a broad direction set already and all you can do is decide how you want to experience the journey. So we did this.

    At the end of the 2022/23 football season, (another injury ravaged, stress filled one for Liverpool FC that left our actual business in near financial ruin), I took a couple of weeks off. No more distractions. What had begun as a typing up, became a polish, became a pseudo-collaboration. Me, aged forty, writing shoulder to shoulder with a thirty-something year old version of my Dad. Time Travel? Time Travel. Sort of. Taking a significant bulk of what was already there, adding in my childhood imaginings of the locations, the characters and stories, and then adding some of my own modern takes and experiences to form this finished version. The ending is one of the results of this mashup. In my memory of the story, and then even in later readings, to my mind Andy had always stayed on with Fedora. For Jo, the story pulled her away from the life she wanted to lead, for Andy it showed him the life he'd always wanted to lead but only could in his dreams. In the original draft it's a little more open ended, and perhaps a little thin too. The last chapter was very short, almost a tad-rushed, it felt like a sprint to the finish line. As it was written with a competition deadline in mind this was very much the case. One of the things I was keen to do was slow things down, keep the pacing, let the characters breathe and hopefully give them a more satisfying conclusion. In September 2023, I took my Dad for a cold, overpriced but ultimately lovely pint at the Elephant Pub in Woolton Village and explained to him what my "Plan" was. We spoke about the origins of the book, the inspirations and eventually got onto original thoughts and plans for the characters. Though it wasn't really there on the page, in his head he'd envisaged that Andy would come back and maybe be rehomed with a new family, and get a more stable life somewhere outside of the city. In my head all I could see was Luke Skywalker in Return of The Jedi. Slightly older, more composed and assured. Dressed in black. The fact that that film was referenced in the coach scene earlier in the book probably fed that vision in my mind's eye too. As a kid Andy was obviously the character I most related to, I loved the idea of him being able to become more, getting a taste of this fantasy life and throwing himself into it. Not just a farm boy from Tatooine, not anymore. Ultimately though I just thought it was cool, I thought my 12 year old son would think so too, and I'm also i'm sucker for sequel bait. But more on that later.

  So anyway yes the pint. Or two. But no more than hree. With a finished manuscript in hand it was time to let the cat out of the bag. The time felt right. In my head we might be able to get it out in time for Christmas (2023). In hindsight Fedora and MIKE would've struggled with such a feat of time manipulation. The biggest delay was the art which to me was almost as important as the story itself. It had to be perfect. As someone who has dedicated nearly fifteen years of his life to Youtube and social media- I can tell you unequivocally that the cover matters. I've seen great content go unseen and crap content mega viral because of the artwork. If I was going to try and get this thing seen by a wider audience, then it needed to stand out. The only man for the job was Yoni Weisberg.

  I'd known Yoni for a few years at this point- I'd commissioned him to do the poster and cover art for Redmen TV's Jordan Henderson documentary and accompanying book. The guy is a genius. He is also, as a result, a man in demand. Over the coming months Yoni, working out of nothing but kindness and a belief in the quality of the story, chipped away at it until he finally unveiled the masterpiece you hold in your hands. In the interim of course I had a couple of cracks at it myself, I owed it to the fifteen year old Paul learning his chops on our Pentium III PC, but yeah nothing quite beats the feeling of handing over a design brief to someone who is brilliant at what they do and then STILL being blown away by the results. It was also his idea to make a Special Edition cover that had the ripped/worn paper effect that paid homage to the original manuscript, and I just LOVE little touches like that. That's the fun stuff. The stuff you only come up with when you are wrist deep in the thing, sleep deprived in the wee hours, and that special kind of madness/delusion/inspiration hits. Love that stuff.

  The other stuff I love is "the process", the nuts and bolts, the early slivers of inspiration that go on to form something greater down the line. I thought that the original typed manuscripts were it, that and the aforementioned pint(s)-driven conversation. But no, it turns out there was more! From out of nowhere, with scant days until we were due to go to print, my Dad drops the (to me anyway) bombshell that he has his original notes, sketches and cuttings from the 80's. Fighting down my first instinct to throttle him for not mentioning this sooner, I am soon lost in a stack of handwritten sheets of paper and the treasure trove of "Man Who" related trivia. For those interested, I've included some of this in the pages that follow. Maybe I'm the only one who cares, maybe not, but it's there regardless, a little time capsule of the mid-80's. There's a chance a three or four year old me was in the room when it was being written. Were the tea stains my fault? I choose to think so.

     Anyway, circling back around. The ending. Yep, as my Dad has already written, he was very, VERY ahead of his time with so many elements of predicting the sci-fi and media trends of the decades that would follow, but foreseeing that the England Women's team would win the Euros? Sadly not. That would've meant his true calling lay elsewhere, a much more financial comfortable elsewhere! No, that bit was me. Why? For a few reasons. One, I thought that for a young woman who was desperately trying to make her way as a footballer, that she would take a great deal of encouragement from knowing that the Women's game had a bright future. Secondly, I thought it was a nice uplifting moment to end on. BUT ALSO, I have an idea for how Andy's message could resonate even more in future stories.
     Yes, future stories. There, I said it. It's said.

What shape will they take? Will MY son be the one polishing stuff off in another forty years? I hope not. There have been conversations. In my head there are at least two more parts, because all good time travel stories need sequels right? We've got the characters, they've got a TIME MACHINE, they can go anywhere! What happens to Fedora's quest to restore football in her world? Why is Andy older? What happened to him after Jo left Limbo? Will MIKE ever find a suitable acronym? Does Fedora have a surname or is the single name-thing a Pele/Madonna homage? All good questions, thanks for asking them.

For now though I hope you have enjoyed this ride, both inside the book and outside in the real world, it has been a genuinely life changing experience, and before I leave you with some of the bonus content I would like to offer my sincere thanks to everyone who has helped us will this thing into existence. Of course the Kickstarter backers, many of whom are listed in these pages, but also to everyone who donated, or just sent in kind words of support, both for the project and for my Mum's health. We launched the Kickstarter at 9am on a Thursday. It had beaten its target by 3pm. I cried three times that day.

Dementia is truly, truly, incomprehensibly dreadful and it has been quite humbling to hear stories from so many other people who have gone through/are going through something similar. Huge strides have been taken and there's a chance that future generations won't have to suffer through this, but right now there is no cure. What we have achieved here could never therefore be that. What we HAVE done is given a wonderful, selfless and (to me certainly) inspirational man a chance to fulfil a dream, and in the process we've hopefully given he and my Mum the financial freedom to spend their remaining time together any way they see fit.

Thank you all so much. See you all again in the future.

Paul - July 2024.

BONUS CONTENT

THE UNUSED COVERS:

One of my most singular obsessions since the late 90's has been to give the book as striking a front cover as possible. Included here is the evolution of that beginning first with my own (distinctly less capable) attempts to create something suitable.

LEFT: The original photoshop layout with all my "borrowed" character models. Yes, those are my arms in a Christmas jumper. Yes, that is Jennifer Holland. Yes, that is Hugh Jackman from Logan.

RIGHT: My amateurish efforts to do it all myself. I showed this to Yoni, who was very polite in that he didn't laugh in my face, and managed to incorporate a few of these elements into the final piece.

One thing in particular that we pivoted away from was the England connection, which was a shame as that "shocked Bobby Moore" image had been burned into my brain since childhood. But, given our connection to the Liverpool FC "scene", Yoni, my Dad and I all felt it best to lean more Scouse than English.

LEFT: Another idea that I was messing around with. I wanted something that could work as an interior title page in black and white, and then it kind of grew out from there. The obvious question? Where did the glasses come from? It's a very good question.

RIGHT: Time was running tight to launch the Kickstarter, and with Yoni up against the clock, this was my fallback in case we needed to press Go on the campaign before he was done. Not sure we would have gotten away with the (even heavily stylised) Spidey in there!

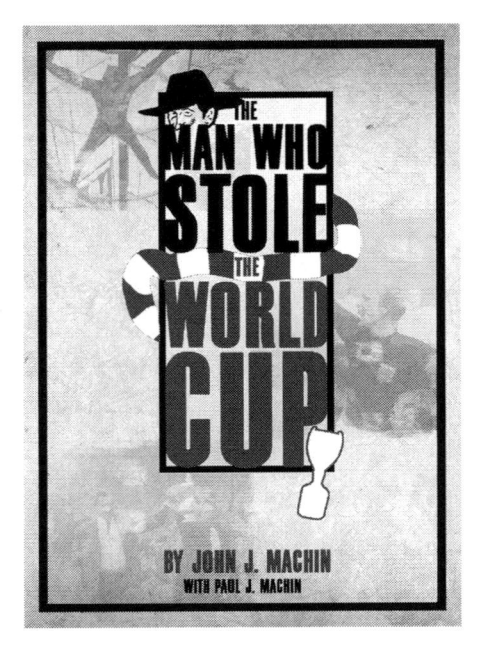

THE YONI WEISBERG COVERS:

I've said it elsewhere, but from the moment this project started to take shape, Yoni was my number one choice. He is, as you will have seen from the finished piece, an absolute genius. Our early discussions centred around the idea of making it like a classic 80's movie poster, like Indiana Jones or Star Wars- allowing us to show the characters but also give a flavour of the story too.

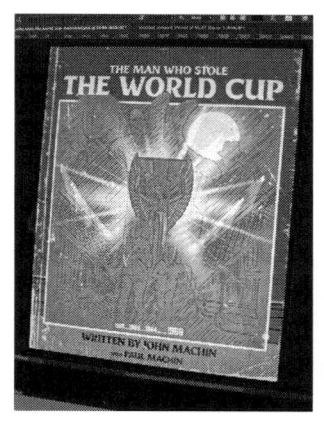

LEFT: A really cool, 70's/80's pulp novel inspired cover mockup. This was something that Yoni did in various forms throughout the process, allowing us all to visualise it more as a finished piece.

RIGHT: The first sketch. It's funny to look back on, seeing this for the first time was such a pivotal moment. My Dad text me his reaction: "Brilliant. Got quite emotional there for a minute."

BONUS CONTENT

BELOW: One of the work in progress updates. As you can see, the details for Fedora, Jo and Andy were starting to take shape. The main difference here of course is in the title/font. My main note on here was asking if we could homage the Amazing Spider-man font instead, which ultimately he absolutely nailed- more on that in a minute. The other notes where about Andy's hair (too long), giving him a jacket and also giving Jo a scarf around her wrist.

THE MAN WHO STOLE THE WORLD CUP

WRITTEN BY JOHN MACHIN WITH PAUL MACHIN

BONUS CONTENT

PREVIOUS PAGE: The Kickstarter Launch Version. We had decided that in order to give the project the best possible chance then we needed to launch before the end of the 2023/24 football
season. With time running tight, Yoni and I made the call to run with a more simplified version of the cover. With the detail work on Jo, Andy and the Trophy done, they became the strong centre of the piece which gave him time to finish off the other elements. It's funny, I still look at this, even it's it's unfinished state and am blown away by how good it is. There is one glaring error though. Have you spotted it? I certainly didn't, credit for that goes to my wife Charlie. Yep, the 2nd "The" is missing from the title. Yoni and I had a little giggle about that one. Still it's so good i'm not sure anyone else actually noticed.

ABOVE: The Kickstarter cover image. As you can see, the spelling error? (spelling *omission??*) Made it into the campaign, though I tried my best to hide it with the central image. Another little aside on this is that the wording is actually correct on the spine of the mockup image.

OTHER COVER BITS:

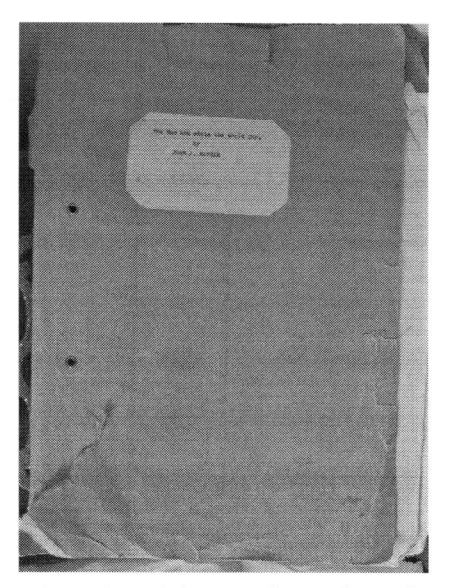

LEFT: The Original typed manuscript. There are two copies of this in existence but this is the only one which has the name of the book and the author printed on the label. The other (which I used for all of the Kickstarter promotion before discovering this fact) is actually blank.

BELOW: The pre-launch Kickstarter header image with Yoni's first sketch and my attempt at a cover mockup. If we'd had to launch a week earlier this is what it would have had to look like. Basically much worse!

THE 1987 DRAFT FILES
During the final process of putting this book together we were able to find not just my Dad's typed manuscripts for the book, but also his original handwritten notes, AND a full hand written maunscript version too, something I had until that point never actually seen before. The following pages contains some of the best pieces of that content.

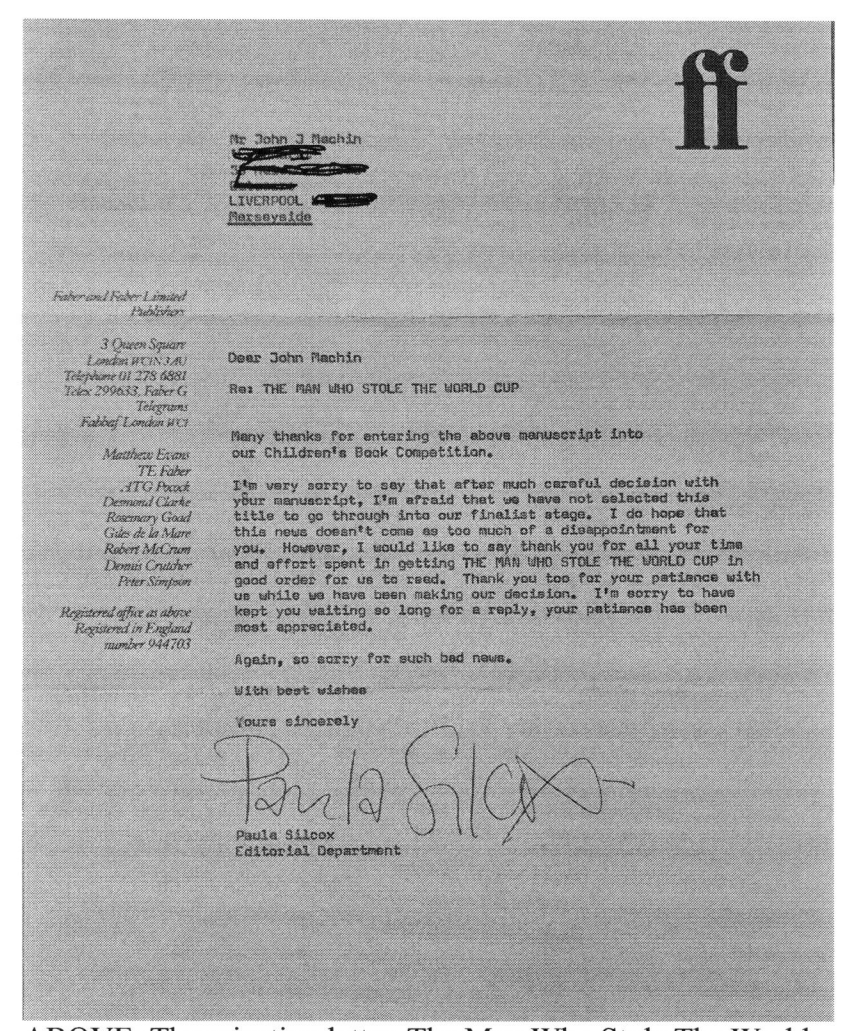

ABOVE: The rejection letter. The Man Who Stole The World Cup was originally created as an entry to a publisher's competition looking for new children's books. Sadly it wasn't chosen. Maybe it did in an alternate universe?

BONUS CONTENT

Behold the height of 80's image reproduction technology, the almighty photocopier! Top Left: ASM 121 (spoilers, the one where Gwen dies); Top Right: The Number 1. Below: John's pencil sketch of the fans in the late 1800's watching the match from the trees, copied from an original reference pic.

John's handwritten notes for the Hooliganism chapter and his little doodle of the original FA Cup too. There's mention here of the player being rewarded with pints of Guinness, that didn't make it into the story.

BONUS CONTENT

Notes taken from a newspaper report on the theft of the Jules Rimet Trophy. The dust sheets, the "slim, sallow complexion" of the suspect as well as the Methodist Service taking place were all historically accurate additions. The asthmatic old security guard was probably doing the "leading security" a disservice mind you.

200

ABOVE: Notes from a pre-draft visit to the Methodist Hall in London.
NEXT PAGE: The text from a plaque on site noting it as the location for the first ever meeting of the United Nations.
BOTTON: Alternative Timelines!!

CENTRAL HALL
TO.
The Glory of God
And In
Prayer for Peace on Earth
This tablet Commemorates
The First Meeting
of the
General Assembly
of the
UNITED NATIONS
in the
Methodist Central Hall
Westminster
Jan 10 – Feb 14 1946.

Plaque on left side wall (if facing front door.)

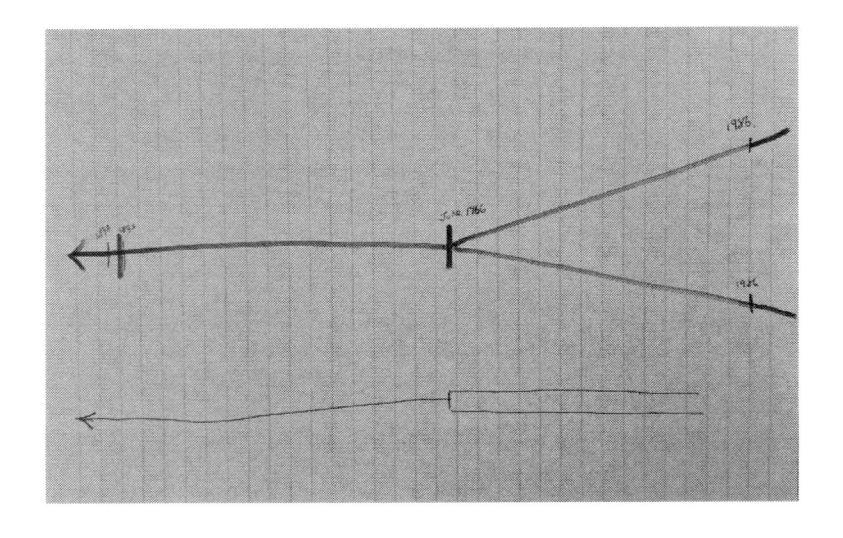

A very early page of notes outlining the kids' characters. At this stage they were both going to be boys (and were only identified as A and B. One, a young delinquent who loved football and the other an abused child who loved comic books. As you can see, most of these traits were eventually folded into Andy's character.

BONUS CONTENT

Further early expansion on the premise of the story. You can see the basic plot points from the opening chapters are here (going to London for the Semi-Final/the Comic Mart, the Man in Black explaining the multi-verse paradox. Again you can see that the kids are both boys at this point, and it feels like Fedora (as yet unnamed) might be an actual man too.

204

A full page story plan. The kids now have names, but Jo is actually "Joe"- presumeably still a boy at this juncture. Also note the mention of "R" which was the pre-feminine name for Fedora's character. Please don't tell any alt-right commentators about the eventual gender swaps! Also there's mention of an Anfield scene that never made it to page.

EVOLUTION:

From Notes To Draft To Print

A look at the creative process for Chapter One: Kenny Dalglish and The Amazing Spider-man. The following pages show the various drafts that the book went through to reach this finalised stage. The Four Versions included are:

1) The Original Handwritten Draft: This was the very first time that the story was committed to paper.

2) The "Best" Handwritten Draft: This is the 2nd handwritten version- done in John's best hand-writing so that it could be typed up.

3) The Type-writer Manuscript: The first proper manuscript version put to paper via the medium on a typewriter.

4) The 2023 Manuscript: The newly polished version created on Google Docs and printed out by computer (because it seems insane to do this on a typewriter in the 21st Century.

THE MAN WHO STOLE THE WORLD CUP

Chapter One: Kenny Dalglish and The Amazing Spiderman
FRIDAY
APRIL 4th 1986: 12.38 p.m.

"If you could make a wish what would you wish for?"

"I thought you always got three wishes? I read this comic once where this astronaut landed on..."

"Alright, three then."

"It's alright, I only need one." Andy said seriously. "I wish I had superpowers."

"Superpowers!" Jo's voice rose with incredulity and rang around the empty top deck of the bus.

"So? what's wrong with that? I'd be dead strong, an' I'd be able to fly or jump from tall buildings and I'd be able to read minds and make people do what I said an..."

Jo laughed — "you're crackers!"

"No I'm not," Andy said with a touch of hurt in his voice. "I'd be able to do whatever I wanted, go anywhere and I'd be famous." He paused. Jo looked at him, "Go on then, what about you?" he asked finally.

"Me?" said Jo with mock surprise. "O, I wish I was Kenny Dalglish, the best footballer in the world."

"Kenny Dalglish? But you're a girl!"

"So?" She turned and glared at him. "What's that got to do with it? I'm a better footballer than you'll ever be."

"Ye' not. I've even played for our school team."

"Get lost." Jo sneered, "your only ten. They don't have school teams that young."

"Yes they do. And I'm eleven."

"No they don't. And you're not."

"Yes they do, and i'll be next week. What would you know about it anyway." Andy was about to add again that Jo was only a girl but seeing the aggression on her face thought better of it. "They certainly don't have any in that..."

"You're in..." Jo sneered.

207

BONUS CONTENT

"I can play better than anyone in my school team" Jo said,

"They keep getting beat", she added sadly, her anger dissipating.

"And they still won't play me." Her disgust was clear. "Now if I was Kenny, they'd be begging me."

"O don't start that again."

"I'm serious"

"Ye' sure"

"Honest haven't you ever wished you could be someone else (just for a bit until everyone realised how good you were) just so you could show people."

"Ye'"

"Well?... Who?... Well what?... Well who?"

"Peter Parker."

"Peter Parker who's he when he's at home."

"Peter Parker The Amazing Spiderman!"

"The Amazing Spiderman?" Jo laughed again. "You must be joking."

"No I'm not. It's no worse than a girl wanting to be Kenny Dalglish."

"Don't start me" — Jo's anger returned

"well it's not."

"But the Amazing whatsaname? He's not even real."

"What's that got to do with it? Besides he's more real than other superheroes. He's got problems with his Aunt, who he lives with, and with his girlfriend and everything. Just like anyone. But he's also got this power 'cause he was bitten by a radioactive spider. He can climb walls and swing around the city. And he's always catching colds and getting beat up and

THE MAN WHO STOLE THE WORLD CUP

"It's what superheroes do, caught villains and crooks," Jo interrupted cynically.

"Funny! Doesn't sound weird to me, shouldn't he catch villains not crooks. He always wins in the end and all the people who think he's little and young..."

"Like you," Jo laughed.

"Shut up. Anyway no one suspects who he really is. Except for his girlfriend's dad but he gets killed when Doc Octopus drops a brick wall on him and Gwendy, that's the daughter she thinks Spiderman did it and hates him 'cause she doesn't know he's really J.S."

"O.K. O.K. I get the picture. He's got problems. But Kenny really is real. He's realer than whatsisname."

"More real."

"What?"

"More real not realer."

"Right, smart alec, more real."

"But you're never goin' to be him are you. I mean Girls don't play football."

"Yes they do. There's girls! women teams all over Europe. They even play in the same stadiums as the men's teams and they earn lots of money."

"Go 'way. They do and most of the best women footballers are from England. There aren't many teams here so they have to go abroad. That's what I'm going to do. I'm gonna go to Italy and play in Rome where the glorious Reds won two European Cups. I'm gonna be the female Kenny Dalglish. Where are you gonna find a radio-active spider?" Jo laughed again.

"Go on laugh. Strange things have happened. They happen all the time."

"Like what?"

"Flying Saucers. Aliens from outer Space."

"Go 'way. You don't believe in that rubbish do

you.
"Ye'. It's a well known fact. The army just keep the evidence a secret so as not to scare people."
"My Aunty — he continued — told me she saw a flying saucer by the shops in Page Moss once and not long after that our teacher told us she'd seen the same one so it must be true.
"Honest?" The мненияof adults added weight to the story.
"Ye'. There's nothing to stop us seeing one now."
"O ye' don't think we will do yer," Jo said peering around. "I'd die!"
"There are lots of stories of people being taken up into space crafts and aliens experimenting on them. Weeks later they are found wandering around suffering from radiation burns and when they are hypnotised they remember everything."
"Oooo that's horrible. Fancy having slimy hands all over you. Ugh!" Andy said indignantly.
"There at slimy! They're like us only either shorter or much taller depending on which kind they are. Now if one came now and tried to use it's beam to raise us up into the ship but the machine broke down so that we blinked in and out of our space and time and then the ship escaped I could end up with all sorts of powers. So could you."
"I think I'd rather be Kenny Dalglish. Anyway I think you've been reading too many comics."
"I collect them."
"What? Comics?"
"Ye'."
"What for?"
"'Cause I like them. And there worth lots of money. Yes only better on an Amazing Spiderman N°1 costs as much as £200.

THE MAN WHO STOLE THE WORLD CUP

"You're jokin'. Have you got one?"
"No. No such luck. I've got them all from Number 121 when Gwendy gets killed by the Green Goblin."
"You what?"
"Gwendy — Spidey's girlfriend."
"Spare me the details. How much is that worth?"
"O about £6."
"You paid £6 for a comic."
"No. I only paid 10p in a junk shop!"
"Wow! When are you selling it?"
"Sell it? I'm not gonna sell it."
"Well what's the point?"
"Point? There isn't one. I just like comics I told you and besides I want to get all of them first — of Spiderman I mean."
"I always heard you were a bit of a brain box."
"Can't see it myself you're daft. Comics!!"
"That's why I absconded from the Assessment Centre."
"You what? You're on the run?"
"Yes. There's a comic mart in London tomorrow. I've got to go. They don't have them in Liverpool anymore and they're bound to have loads of old spidey's."
"I thought you said they were expensive. Where are you getting the money?"
"Well. Something will come up. Yes. Isn't stealing what got you into the Remand Home in the first place. It's an Assessment Centre at present. What else can they do to me?"
"And how are you getting down there? It's two hundred miles away."
"I thought I'd go with you."
"Me?"   "So?"
"Yes. You're going to the match aren't you. The Semi-Final of the F.A. Cup. Liverpool versus Southampton. White Hart Lane, Tottenham. London. Kenny Dalglish."

211

I'm not entirely sure what my favourite thing about this version is. It probably should be how close it is to being the finished version straight off the bat, but in reality i'm torn between it being the tea stains on the first few pages or the fact that Andy uses the expression "absconded from" rather than "did a runner from" as in later drafts.

THE MAN WHO STOLE THE WORLD CUP

Chapter 1.

KENNY DALGLISH AND THE AMAZING SPIDERMAN.

FRIDAY. 4TH APRIL 1986. 12.38 p.m.

"If you could make a wish what would it be?" The teenage girl, pulled a pink plastic comb through her shoulder-length brown hair and looked out of the bus window as if uninterested in the answer.

"I thought you always got three wishes?" The young boy suggested fidgetting on the cold vinyl seat. "I read this comic once where this astronaut landed on ...."

"Alright three then." This time Jo looked at him.

"Its alright I only need one." Andy said seriously. "I wish I had super-powers."

"Superpowers?!" Jo's voice rose with incredulity and rang around the empty top deck.

"Je' what's wrong with that? I'd be dead strong, and I'd be able to fly, or jump tall buildings and I'd be able to read minds and make people do whatever I said an' ...."

Jo laughed and tossed back her head. "You're crackers."

"No I'm not," Andy said with a touch of hurt in his voice. "I'd be able to do whatever I wanted, go anywhere and, and I'd be famous." He paused. "What about you?"

"Me?" said Jo with mock surprise. "O I wish I was Kenny Dalglish, the best footballer in the world."

"Kenny Dalglish? But you're a girl!"

"So?" She turned and glared at him. "What's that got to do with it? I'm a better footballer than you'll ever be."

"Yer not. I've even played for our school team."

"Get lost." Jo sneered returning the comb to her hair. "Your only ten. They don't have school teams that young."

"Yes they do. And I'm eleven."

"No they don't and you're not."

BONUS CONTENT

"They do and I will be next week. What would you know about it anyway you're only a......" Andy was about to add again that she was only a girl but seeing the aggression on her face thought better of it.

Jo was less thoughtful. "They certainly don't have any teams in that Remand Home you're in anyhow," she sneered and added. "I can play better than anyone in my school team."

She looked wistfully out of the window. "They keep getting beat," she said. "And they still don't play me!" Her disgust was clear. "Now if I was Kenny they'd be begging me."

"O don't start that again," Andy sighed.

"I'm serious."

"Ye' sure."

"Honest. Haven't you ever wished you could be someone else — just so you could show people?"

"Yes."

"Well?"

"Well what?"

"Well who?"

"Peter Parker."

"Peter Parker. Who's he when he's at home?"

"Peter Parker, the Amazing Spiderman!" Andy announced dramatically.

"The Amazing Spiderman?" Jo laughed. "You must be joking."

"No I'm not. It's no worse than a girl wanting to be Kenny Dalglish."

"Don't start me." Jo stabbed the handle of the comb at Andy's shoulder.

"Well it's not."

"But the Amazing Whatsaname? He's not even real."

"What's that got to do with it? Besides he more real than other superheroes. He's got problem with his aunt, who he lives with, and with his girlfriend and everything. Just like anyone. But he's also got this power 'cause he was bitten by a radio-active spider. He can climb walls and swing around the city on his webbing...". Andy paused for breath ... "and he's always catching colds and getting beaten up and ...."

"I thought superheroes caught villains not colds," Jo interrupted, smiling.

"Fun—ny!" Andy pulled a face and continued. "He always wins in the end and all the people who think he's little and puny..."

"Like you," Jo laughed.

"Shut up. Anyway no one suspects who he really is, except for his girlfriend's dad but he gets killed when Doc. Octopus drops a brick wall on him and Gwendy, that's the girlfriend, she thinks Spiderman did it and hates him 'cause she doesn't know he's really..."

"O.K. O.K I get the picture" Jo interrupted the torrent. "So he's got problems. But Kenny really is real. He's realer than whatsisname."

"More real," Andy corrected.

"What?"

"More real not realer."

"Alright smart aleck, more real"

"But you're never going to be him are you. I mean girls don't play football."

"Yes they do. There's women teams all over Europe. They even play in the same stadiums as the men's teams and they earn lots of money."

"Go 'way."

"They do and most of the best women players are from England, like me. There aren't many teams here so they have to go abroad. That's what I'm going to do. I'm gonna go to Italy and play in Rome where the glorious Reds won two European Cups. I'm gonna be the female Kenny Dalglish. Where are you gonna find a radio-active spider?" Jo laughed again.

BONUS CONTENT

"Go on laugh. Stranger things have happened." Andy insisted and brushed his hand across his bristly crew cut. "They happen all the time."

"Like what?"

"Flying Saucers for one. Aliens from Outer Space."

"Get away. You don't believe in that rubbish do you?"

"Ye'. It's a well known fact," Andy said authoritatively. "The army just keep the evidence a secret so as not to scare people."

"Behave." Jo sneered but there was doubt in her voice.

"My Aunty saw one by Page Moss shops, she told me and not long after that our teacher told us she had seen the same one, so it must be true."

"Honest?" The mention of adults added weight to the story.

"Ye'." Andy continued " there's nothing to stop us seing one now."

"O you doi't think we will do ye'." Jo grabbed the boys arm and peered out at the sky. "I'd die."

"There are lots of stories of people being taken up into Space Crafts and the aliens experimenting on them. Weeks later they turn up and have radiation burns all over them and don't remember anything until they're hypnotised."

"Ooow! That's horrible." Jo shivered and squirmed visibly. "Fancy having slimy hands all over you. Urgh!"

"They are not slimy." Andy said indignantly. "They're like us only either shorter or much taller depending on which kind they are. Now, if one came now and tried to use its tractor beam to raise us up into the ship but the machine broke down so that we blinked in and out of our space and time and then got left behind as the saucer escaped. I could end up with all sorts of powers. So could you."

"I think I'd rather be Kenny Dalglish. Anyway I think you've been reading too many comics. This is my stop."

THE MAN WHO STOLE THE WORLD CUP

5

They left the bus together, and as they dodged their way through the lunch time city crowds Andy found himself a step behind watching his companion.

She was dressed in a dark blue, fashion leather jacket, jeans with one inch turn ups, a deep red blouse with all but its pointed collar hidden by a pale brown hand knitted jumper. Low heeled, shiny black shoes completed the outfit.

She carried a rolled up magazine in her right hand which accentuated the downward punching motion she made alternately with each fist as she walked.

This affected movement made it more of a strut than a walk, full of pride and arrogance but also, as was shown by the little skips she made as she left or climbed a kerb, full of joy. When she reached a stretch of waste land full of obstacles, half-bricks, stones and rubbish, she appeared to dance her way through them.

Andy gave a skip himself and landed beside her.

"I collect them," he announced.

"What?" Jo looked at him bewildered.

"Comics."

"Comics?"

"Ye'"

"What for?"

"Because I like them," Andy explained. "And they're worth lots of money."

"What do you mean? Like old football programmes?"

"Yes only better. A Spiderman Number One costs as much as £200."

"You're joking?" Jo lost Andy in the crowd momentarily. "Have you got one?" she reappeared.

"No. No such luck. I've got them all from number 121 when Gwendy gets killed by the Green Goblin."

"You what?"

"Gwendy — I've told you Spidey's girlfriend".

217

"Spare me the details," Jo said haughtily. "How much is that worth?"

"O about £6."

"You paid £6 for a comic?"

"No. I only paid ten p in a junk shop." Andy explained proudly.

"Wow!" Jo was impressed. "When are you selling it?"

"Sell it?" Andy was clearly shocked by the idea. "I'm not gonna sell it."

"Well, what's the point?" Jo was clearly perplexed.

"Point? There isn't one. I just like comics I told you and besides I want to get all of them first — of Spiderman I mean."

"I always heard you were a bit of a brainbox. Can't see it myself, you're daft." Jo shook her head. "Comics!!"

"That's why I did a runner from the Assessment Centre."

"You what?" Jo stopped in her tracks. "You're on the run?"

"Yes. There's a Comic Mart in London tomorrow. I've got to go. They don't have them in Liverpool anymore and they're bound to have loads of old spideys." Andy tried to explain it.

"I thought you said they were expensive," Jo asked her suspicions raised. "Where are you getting the money?"

"Well. Something will come up."

"O yes. Isn't stealing what got you locked up in the first place?"

"Ye' well what can they do to me now?"

"And how are you getting down there? It's two hundred miles away."

"I thought I'd go with you."

"Me?" Jo couldn't believe it.

"Yes. You're going the match aren't you?"

"So?"

> "The Semi-Final of the F.A. Cup," Andy said dramatically. "Liverpool versus Southampton, White Hart Lane, Tottenham, London. Kenny Dalglish."
>
> "I should have known it was no coincidence you bumping into me like this. The answer's no!"
>
> "Please!"
>
> "No! There is no way I'm going to help you bunk on my coach to London. Me dad would murder me!"
>
> "It's alright," Andy explained, "I've got money I just want someone to go with. The police are sure to pick me up if they see me on my own. Our Sandra told me you were going down to the coach station this morning to book for you and your dad. If I book at the same time, I'll get the same coach and it won't look a bit suspicious. I could even sit next to you."
>
> "Well-ll." Jo thought about it.
>
> "Go on..." Andy pleaded "...please."
>
> "O. Alright. My dad and uncle always ignore me anyway. At least it'll give me someone to talk to, though what I'm going to talk to a ten year old kid about I don't know."

A few differences in this one, which I've included for two reasons. The first is to highlight the absolutely (to my modern sensibilties anyway) madness of writing books in the pre-digital era. The idea that you would write the thing, and then literally write the thing out again in full fills me with a cold dread! The other, more frivolous reason is that I love that you can see how much more time consuming and deliberate this version is, that overbearing knowledge that any mistake here is going to be translated in to the typed version. Very cool.

219

BONUS CONTENT

Chapter 1
Kenny Dalglish And The Amazing Spiderman

<u>Friday. 4th April 1986. 12.38 p.m.</u>

"If you could make a wish what would it be?" The teenage girl pulled a pink plastic comb through her shoulder-length brown hair and looked out of the bus window as if uninterested in the answer.

"I thought you always got three wishes?" The young boy suggested, fidgeting on the cold vinyl seat. "I read this comic once where this astronaut landed on......."

"Alright three then." This time Jo looked at him.

"It's alright, I only need one," Andy said seriously. "I wish I had super-powers."

"Superpowers?!" Jo's voice rose with incredulity and rang around the empty top deck.

"Ye' what's wrong with that? I'd be dead strong, and I'd be able to fly, or jump tall buildings and I'd be able to read minds and make people do whatever I said an'...."

Jo laughed and tossed back her head. "You're crackers."

"No I'm not," Andy said with a touch of hurt in his voice. "I'd be able to do whatever I wanted, go anywhere and...and I'd be famous." He paused. "What about you?"

"Me?" said Jo with mock surprise. "O I wish I was Kenny Dalglish, the best footballer in the world."

"Kenny Dalglish? But you're a girl!"

"So?" She turned and glared at him. "What's that got to do with it? I'm a better footballer than you'll ever be."

"Yer not. I've even played for our school team."

"Get lost," Jo sneered, returning the comb to her hair. 'You're only ten. They don't have school teams that young."

THE MAN WHO STOLE THE WORLD CUP

"Yes they do. And I'm eleven."

"No they don't and you're not."

"They do and I will be next week. What would you know about it anyway, you're only a......." Andy was about to add again that she was only a girl, but seeing the aggression on her face thought better of it.

Jo was less thoughtful. "They certainly don't have any teams in that Remand Home you're in anyhow," she sneered and added, "I can play better than anyone in my school team."

She looked wistfully out of the window. "They keep getting beat," she said. "And they still don't play me!" Her disgust was clear. "Now if I was Kenny they'd be begging me."

"O don't start that again," Andy sighed.

"I'm serious."

"Ye' sure."

"Honest. Haven't you ever wished you could be someone else - just so you could show people?"

"Yes."

"Well?"

"Well what?"

"Well who?"

"Peter Parker."

"Peter Parker. Who's he when he's at home?"

"Peter Parker, the Amazing Spiderman!" Andy announced dramatically.

"The Amazing Spiderman?" Jo laughed. "You must be joking."

"No I'm not. It's no worse than a girl wanting to be Kenny Dalglish."

"Don't start me," Jo stabbed the handle of the comb at Andy's shoulder.

BONUS CONTENT

Chapter 1: Kenny Dalglish and the Amazing Spider-man
Friday. 4th April 1986. 12:38pm. Liverpool.

"If you could make a wish, what would it be?" The teenage girl asked as she finished pulling a pink plastic comb through her thick, shoulder length brown hair. She tied it up into a high ponytail using a bright, aqua blue scrunchy, all the while staring out of the bus window, as if uninterested in the answer.

"I thought you always got three wishes?" The young boy suggested, fidgeting on the cold vinyl seat. "I read this comic once where this astronaut landed on…"

"Alright, THREE then." This time Jo turned away from her condensation-obscured view of the outside world to look at him. "Three wishes Andy. What are they?"

"It's sound, I only need one," Andy said cheerfully. "I wish I had super powers."

"Superpowers?!" Jo's voice rose with incredulity and rang around the top deck. At the front of the bus an elderly lady with a paisley patterned head scarf half turned her head back towards the pair, 'harrumphed' in annoyance, and tucked her polythene shopping bag closer to her on the seat. Jo winced, and though she couldn't make it out, was convinced that the old dear was muttering *something* derogatory about them under her breath. She resolved to keep her voice down. Andy however met her tone and ran with it, standing up, and speaking with his hands to further illustrate his impassioned response.

"Yeah! What's wrong with that?? I'd be dead strong, and I'd be able to fly, or jump tall buildings, or climb walls..." He jumped onto the metal bar top of the seat next to them, wobbling slightly, and grabbed the vertical bar for balance. The old woman shifted round in her seat again, Jo's eyes widened in horror, "Andy get off there you little idiot!" She reached out to pull him down, but he skillfully sidestepped and swung acrobatically to the seat across the aisle.

"... I'd be able to read minds, " he continued, putting his right hand to his temple, and his left outstretched in front, "and make people do whatever I want," he pretended to focus, closing his eyes and pointing towards the disgruntled pensioner currently glowering at them from behind her horn rimmed spectacles. "I command you to stop being such a miserable old busybody," he said in a voice much deeper than his own. Jo gritted her teeth. Andy opened one eye to see if his word had any effect, and was met only by the woman's continued death stare. Andy wiggled his fingers and tilted his head back, "I command THEEEEE". The woman let out another large "harrumph," scooped up her bag, and walked down the

And lastly my own efforts. As I've said previously, so much of this book has taken on a life of it's own in my brain since childhood. The characters and places were so vivid to me. My mission was to try and convert those childhood flourishes/head canon into something that enriched the text.

BONUS CONTENT

THE MESSAGE...

> Dear Jurgen,
>
> I don't need to tell you that top line managers are judged by the trophies they win.
>
> However on Merseyside you will be judged by something completely different.
>
> I am old enough to remember the joy, pride and optimism brought to us by Shankly, Paisley and Kenny.
>
> You have brought this back to us and it is for this that you will never be forgotten in Liverpool or wherever Scousers congregate.
>
> Thank you for it all, and good luck and best wishes for you and your family in the future.
>
> Yours,
> John Mackin

One of the amazing moments during the creation of the book was being able to give an early preview copy to departing Liverpool manager Jurgen Klopp. My Dad wrote him a message on the back page, which I was able to get a picture of before handing it over. Here it is in full.

KICKSTARTER BACKERS

As part of the Kickstarter project we offered people a couple of Tiers to get their names in the book. These are the names of those wonderful people who took that option.

SUPER SUPPORTERS:

**Its__steveo - Andy "Scoop" Davies - Alison Hawkes
Diana & Martin Williams - Michael McCannon**

Sowjana	Andrew Butler
Sam Wright	Jack Hon
Shane Rogers	Jeremy Pryce
Ken Cotter	Toby Owen
Aidan Woodhead	Nigel G G James
Ian Maloy	Jono Vandenberg
Julian Alexander Backhouse	Caleb Cartmel
Darren Lyne	Matt Froud
Luca Grass	Quadbod
Joe J Atkins	Christian Vincent Carpenter
Chris Shepherd	Josh Mierop
Ian Fletcher	David Lever
Ben Prior	Neil Roskell
Andrew Genuardi	Ian M Hartery
Mark Weldon	David Williams
Owen Farrington	Adam Murphy
Cian Crowdy	Olivia Evans
Even Kjellevold	Seamus Smith
Thomas McCarthy	Richard Hughes
Paul M Smith	Dave Kinsella
Peter Abernethy	Will Rubenstein
Geoff Tordzro-Taylor	Jonathan Watson

Kent Murray
Penny Carey
Terry McIvor
Brian (Brace) Miller
Matt Davies
Dan Boyle
PrimeBrit
Paul Breen
Adrian Cork
Mark Galloway
Ian Bradshaw
Keir Smith
Russell Wemple
William Wai Yiu Wong
Leo Teague
Jan Burke
Paul Rearden
Linda Lee
Daniel Watton
Ankur Arora
Leigha Bouldin
Michael Jan Ferreira
Marybeth Maloy Gebauer
Mark Hesketh
Henry Hesketh
The Chisholm Family
Neil Rawlinson
Harry Dalton
Lee Henwood
David Goulding
Leo Richards
Alan Wootton

Wilfred Galloway
Paddy Slattery
Kevin Harrington
Tom Phillips, YNWA
Ketan Sharma
Ryan Flitcroft
Soumen Saha
Axel Yates
Dominic Wyn Bennett
Ahmad Ragab
Jakob Evans
Joshua Perryman
Dennis Jolley
Azhar Talibi
Robert Taylor
Stephen Monaghan
Cameron Hayes
Marley Peter Jones
Martin Kershaw
Harry James Mccauley
Prakash Patel
Guy Constant
Nia & Gareth
Mark McBride
Mark Vidal
Paul Harwood
Ceri-ann Williams
Kenneth Chay
Danny Kwiatkowski
Orrin O'Neill
Mark Jackson
Hugo Jackson

Sir Brian Burrows
Paul McCormick
Dave Oakley
Evan Keaveney
Janno Siimar
Alan Moynihan
Hunter Rogers
Regina Frank
Chris Torode
Stacey Kesterton
Matt Anderson
Vanessa Taylor
Paul Harvey
Kai Yi Yu
David Jordan
Gail Young
Phil Young

Stuart Humpage
Darren Barton
Brendan Smyth
Hussein Ramadan
Mark O'Toole
Quinn Haynie
Chris Kelly
John Paul Chambers
Stuart Kesting
Bethan- Russet Bradbury
Kevin Lynch
Jimmy Peláez
Steven Barker
Willie Homer
Joe Rushton
Daniel Newman

Special Thanks To
Yoni Weisberg
Charlie, Jack and Penny Machin
Lauren and Taylor Machin
Chris Pajak
Dan Clubbe
Owen Farrington
Carl Woodward
Paul Salt
Neil Atkinson
Craig Houlden
Jurgen Klopp

Love you Mam x

ABOUT THE AUTHORS

JOHN J. MACHIN:

John was born in Liverpool in 1951, and grew up in the Norris Green area of the city. He studied Political Science and Economics at Birmingham University, where he met his future wife Annette. The pair returned to Liverpool after graduation, got married and went into teaching (Annette) and Social Work (John) in 1973 (a big year!). Their first child, Paul was born in 1983, with Lauren following in 1991. John retired from his role as Manager of the Disabled Children's Service in 2012 and since then has taken up Tai Chi, continued his role as the family's Culinary expert, whilst also being an amazing hands-on "Pops" to his three grandkids Jack, Penny and Taylor. A huge Liverpool fan, he spent 20 years standing on the famous Spion Kop and has been an Anfield season ticket holder since the 80's; he also has an amazing archive of Marvel comics dating back to the 60's including a cherished copy of Amazing Spider-man #1.

PAUL J. MACHIN:

Paul is the Founder and Presenter of The Redmen TV, the largest unofficial Liverpool FC channel on Youtube, and the originator of the "Fan Media" movement in football. He has self published four LFC related books, worked as a freelance pundit for Sky Sports, TNT Sports, BBC, ITV, ESPN and CNN, and once hugged Jurgen Klopp. As Watchmen writer Alan Moore once commented, Paul was "brainwashed by John as a child" and therefore shares his deep love for the Superhero genre, as well as Liverpool Football Club. Husband to Charlie and Dad to Jack and Penny, both of whom have been pecking his head as to when the book will finally be finished. Paul prefers DC Comics to Marvel, a fact John describes as "like raising a son to support Everton".

Printed in Great Britain
by Amazon

df22e6e9-b609-43b7-b9fa-40016d6df8b8R01